BEST-LOVED DESIGNERS'
C O L L E C T I O N

Quick-Sew Quilts

Wallhangings and Coordinating Projects
from America's Top Designers

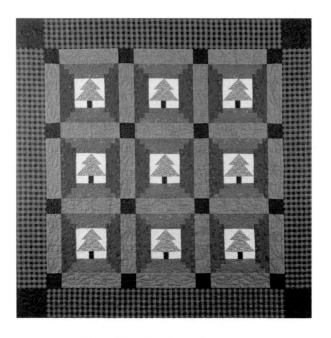

Edited by Becky Johnston

Chilton
BOOK COMPANY

BEST-LOVED DESIGNERS' COLLECTION:
QUICK-SEW QUILTS
Copyright © 1996 by Landauer Corporation

This book was designed and produced by
Landauer Books
A division of Landauer Corporation
12251 Maffitt Road, Cumming, Iowa 50061

President and Publisher: Jeramy Lanigan Landauer
Editor in Chief: Becky Johnston
Art Director: Lyne Neymeyer
Editor: Janet Pittman
Copy Editor: Joanna Heist
Graphic Designer: Nicole Bratt
Photographer: Lyne Neymeyer
Technical Illustrators: Roxanne LeMoine; Lorna Johnson
Creative Associates: Glenda Dawson; Margaret Sindelar
Prepress: Event Graphics
Printed in U.S.A.

Published by Chilton Book Company, Radnor, Pennsylvania

Library of Congress Cataloging-in-Publication Data

Quick-sew quilts: wallhangings and coordinating projects from
 America's top designers/ [Editor, Becky Johnston].—lst ed.
  p. cm.—(Best-loved designers' collection)
  Includes index.
  ISBN 0-8019-8891-8 (pbk. :alk. paper)
  ISBN 0-8019-8928-0 (hdcvr. :alk. paper)
  1. Wall hangings. 2. Patchwork—Patterns. 3. Appliqué—Patterns.
4. Quilts I. Johnston, Becky. II. Series.
TT850.2.Q53 1996
746.46'041—dc20   96-31936
                                                           CIP

This book is printed on acid-free paper.

1 2 3 4 5 6 7 8 9 10   5 4 3 2 1 0 9 8 7 6

Lynette Jensen
Thimbleberries

Margaret Sindelar
Cottonwood Classics

Sandy Belt
Town Folk Designs

Sally Korte & Alice Strebel
Kindred Spirits

Patrice Longmire
Patrice & Co.

McKenna Ryan
Pine Needles

Janet Pittman
Garden Trellis Designs

Cheryl Jukich
Thread Bare Pattern Company

Kris Kerrigan
Button Weeds

Suellen Wassem & Shery Jespersen
Pieceful Heart Designs

Leslie Beck
Fiber Mosaics

INTRODUCTION

Treat yourself to 11 fabulous country and folk art wall quilts using fresh new fabrics, felt, dimensional appliqué, and many exciting embellishments. Then enjoy a bonus collection of 55 sew-simple projects you can finish in a flash!

The 11 contributing artisans are some of the country's best fabric artists who combine the simple charm of folk art with a dash of down-home country to create their unique designs. You'll find them listed here in the order each designer's chapter appears in the book.

In this delightful collection, each chapter opens with a whimsical wall quilt sure to warm heart and home. Charming motifs from each of the featured wallhangings inspire a myriad of coordinating folk art and country projects. Discover fun wearables, wreaths, country critters, greeting cards, Christmas ornaments, decorative home accents, and much more.

To spark your imagination, you'll find dozens of fresh new projects from your favorite designers sprinkled throughout the following pages. We'll show you how to go beyond piecing with the newest and quickest way to quilt using fusible adhesive, then top it all off with imaginative new ways to embellish with floss, felt and flannel, paints and pens, buttons and beads, ribbons, and yo-yos by the yard!

To help you experience the fun of working with new materials and techniques, we've provided several pages of General Instructions, Tips & Techniques, and a Stitch Guide for hand- and machine-embroidery.

As a special bonus, we've included in our Sources helpful product information and the company names and addresses of all the contributing designers so that you may contact each for the special patterns, fabrics and trims that have gained them well-deserved recognition as some of America's Best-Loved Designers!

TABLE OF CONTENTS

General Instructions

For Every Project

As you gather your materials and supplies and begin each project, here are some guidelines you may find helpful:

- The fabric called for in the materials lists is 44" wide lightweight to mediumweight cotton unless otherwise specified.
- Scraps of fabric are intended to be those you have on hand from other projects. If you don't have a particular color or pattern in your scrap basket, you'll only need to purchase ¼ yard pieces or fat-eighths.
- Since many of these projects—such as the featured wallhangings—are decorative items, it's not necessary to pre-wash the fabrics. Pre-wash fabrics for a garment or any piece that will be laundered.
- Materials lists and photographs indicate fabric color and texture for each project, but feel free to coordinate fabrics in your favorite color schemes.
- Cut strips and rectangles with a rotary cutter for speed and accuracy.
- Sew all seams with a ¼" seam allowance, unless noted otherwise. After stitching, press seam allowances to one side, usually toward the darker fabric.

Quick–Sew Appliqué

Trace, apply fusible web, cut, and fuse

- Use regular or heavyweight fusible web as directed in the materials list. Heavyweight fusible web is for projects where the appliqué pieces are not hand- or machine-stitched. Regular fusible web has a lighter coating of adhesive and the appliqué pieces should be hand- or machine-stitched.
- Place the fusible web with the paper side up over the appliqué patterns in this book. Trace the patterns. (The patterns are the reverse of the finished project.) Cut fusible web about ⅛" outside the tracing (Diagram A). To save time, group and trace all patterns to be cut from one fabric about ¼" apart on the fusible web. Cut around the outside of the grouped patterns.
- Referring to the fusible web package directions, fuse the appliqué to the wrong side of the fabric. Cut out on the traced lines (Diagram B). Transfer dashed placement lines to fabric, if necessary.
- Peel off paper backing. Position the appliqué on the background fabric, overlapping pieces at the dashed lines; fuse in place (Diagram C).

Finishing the wallhanging or quilt

Layering

- Cut the backing and batting several inches larger than the quilt top. (The project's directions specify the desired size.)
- Lay the backing on a flat surface with the wrong side up. Secure edges with tape. Center the batting over the backing, smoothing it flat. Position the finished top on the batting.

DIAGRAM A

DIAGRAM B

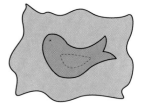

DIAGRAM C

- Hand-baste or safety-pin the layers together, about every 4 inches, beginning in the middle and working to the edges (Diagram D). Trim batting and backing even with or ¼" beyond the edges of the quilt top.

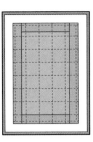
DIAGRAM D

QUILTING

By Machine
- Set the machine for a fairly long straight stitch, and sew along the stitching line. To change direction, move the needle down to secure the fabric, then lift the foot and pivot the fabric on the needle.
- For long parallel lines, sew each row in the same direction.
- For intricate designs, use an embroidery foot attachment and lower the feed dog. Use an embroidery hoop to help keep the fabric stretched.

By Hand
- Thread the needle with an 18" length of quilting thread and tie a small knot at the end of the thread. Insert the needle into the quilt back, about 1" from your quilting line. Bring the needle up at the beginning of the quilting line, giving the thread a gentle tug to pull the knot through the backing so it is hidden in the batting.
- Using small even running stitches, take several stitches at a time. To end off on the back, wind the thread several times around the needle to make a knot close to fabric. Insert needle into fabric, draw the knot into batting, pull needle through fabric about 1" from end of stitching; cut thread.

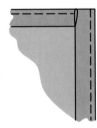
DIAGRAM E

BINDING

Mitered Corners
- Sew the binding strips together into one long strip. Fold and press the strip in half lengthwise with the right side out.
- With raw edges even, pin the binding to the quilt top, leaving several inches of binding loose at the beginning. Sew with a ¼" seam allowance. Stop sewing ¼" from the corner (Diagram E), and remove the quilt from the machine.
- At the corner, fold the binding up at a 45° angle, then down at a 90° angle. Sew from the top (Diagram F), continuing along the edge to 6" from beginning of stitching. Overlap; trim ends to ½". Open binding, sew the ends together, refold binding and finish sewing to the top.
- Turn binding to the back so it just covers the stitching. Whipstitch folded binding edge in place, making mitered corners on the back (Diagram G).

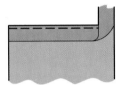
DIAGRAM F

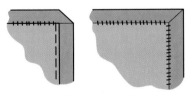
DIAGRAM G

Straight Corners
- Fold and press each binding strip in half lengthwise with the right side out. With raw edges even, pin a strip to the top edge of the quilt; sew with a ¼" seam allowance (Diagram H). Press the strip away from the top. Add a binding strip to the bottom edge, and then to each side edge. Fold the binding to the back and whipstitch in place, covering the stitching.

DIAGRAM H

Lynette Jensen

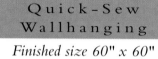

For quilt designer Lynette Jensen, the true joy of her business is that it involves doing exactly what she would choose to do for a hobby.

Her love for the needle-arts, antiques, fabrics, color, and design led her to create a thriving business—Thimbleberries. The company that she started in 1989 with the introduction of four quilt patterns, now features dozens of patterns, numerous books, kits for miniature quilts, and fabrics.

According to Lynette, "I feel that nothing gives a home more individual personality than a variety of needlework, and of course quilts are essential to achieve that inviting comfortable 'country look.' My intent is to offer unique designs that have traditional appeal with easy to follow instructions."

For the wallhanging shown here, Lynette combined two quilt patterns—Courthouse Steps and Pine Tree—to create the Courthouse Pine block.

You'll find the block featured with other motifs in this impressive collection of home-decorating accents designed by Lynette. The projects inspired by the wallhanging use coordinating prints from Thimbleberries' distinctive line of fabrics combined with other quality woven plaids and calicos.

MATERIALS

- ¼ yard each of green and beige print fabrics for trees and background
- ¼ yard each of three red print and three chestnut print fabrics for courthouse steps strips
- ¾ yard of brown print fabric for trunks, sashing blocks, and corner blocks
- 1 yard of green check fabric for sashing
- 1 yard of homespun check (60" wide fabric) for outer border
- 3 yards of fabric for backing
- 66" x 66" piece of batting
- ¾ yard of red print fabric for binding

Quick-Sew Wallhanging

Finished size 60" x 60"

CUTTING

1. Trace patterns on pages 16 and 17. From the green print fabric, cut nine each of templates A and C.
2. From the beige print fabric, cut nine each of B, B-reversed, D, and D-reversed; and two 3" x 20" strips.
3. From the brown print fabric, cut a 1½" x 20" strip for trunks, sixteen 3½" squares for the sashing blocks, and four 6½" squares for the corner blocks.
4. From each of the red print and chestnut print fabrics, cut four 1½" crosswise strips for courthouse steps strips.
5. From the green check fabric, cut twenty-four 3½" x 12½" strips for the sashing.
6. From the homespun check fabric, cut four 6½" crosswise strips for borders.

PIECING

1. Referring to Diagram A, sew B and B reversed to A. Sew D and D-reversed to C. Sew A/B units to top of C/D units. Repeat to make nine trees.

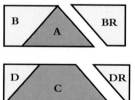

DIAGRAM A

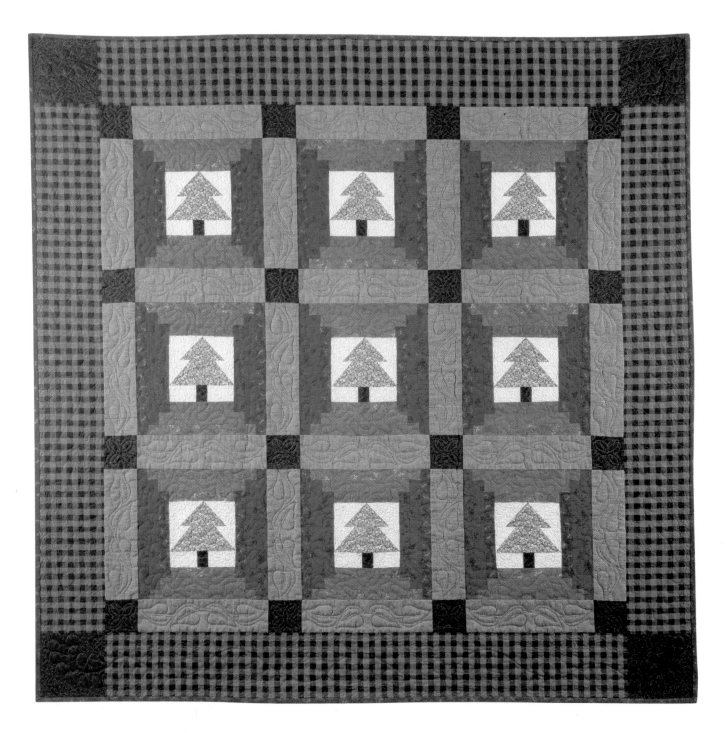

2. Referring to Diagram B, sew a beige strip lengthwise to each side of the brown trunk strip. Crosscut nine 2" wide segments.

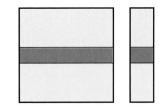

DIAGRAM B

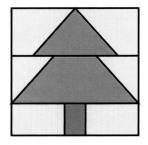

DIAGRAM C

3. Referring to Diagram C, sew trunk unit to bottom of tree unit.

4. Referring to Diagram D, sew courthouse steps strips around each tree block: Sew a chestnut strip to the top and bottom edges; press and trim strips even with block. Sew a red strip to the side edges; press and trim strips even with block. Repeat the sequence, adding two more strips to each side, maintaining the color pattern and the trimming as you go. The finished block should measure 12½" square.

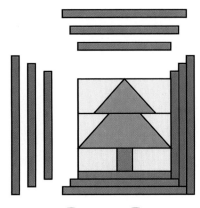

DIAGRAM D

5. Referring to Diagram E, and in alternating order, sew four brown sashing blocks and three green check sashing strips into one long strip; repeat three more times. Sew three tree blocks and four sashing strips into one long strip; repeat two more times. Sew long strips together in alternating order.

6. Measure the quilt top from side to side through the center. Cut two 6½" wide border strips to that measurement.

7. Measure the quilt top from top to bottom through the center. Cut the remaining 6½" wide border strips to that measurement. Add 6½" corner blocks to the ends of these border strips.

8. Sew the shorter strips to the top and bottom edges of the quilt top. Sew the remaining border strips to the sides edges of the quilt top.

FINISHING

1. Refer to General Instructions, page 7, to layer, quilt, and bind the wallhanging.

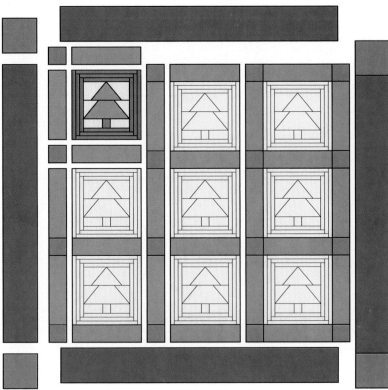

DIAGRAM E

MATERIALS

- Scraps of green, beige, and brown print fabrics for tree, trunk, and background
- Large scraps of chestnut print and red print fabrics for log cabin strips
- ½ yard of checked fabric for border and pillow back
- ⅔ yard of brown print fabric for corner blocks and outer ruffle
- ⅓ yard of red print fabric for inner ruffle
- Scraps of green, red, and gold print fabrics for leaf/stem appliqué and yo-yos
- 18" square each of batting and muslin
- 16" square pillow form

CUTTING

1. Trace patterns on pages 16–17. From green print fabric, cut one each of templates A and C.
2. From beige print fabric, cut one each of templates B, B-reversed, D, and D-reversed; and two 2" x 3" rectangles.
3. From brown print fabric, cut four 3½" squares for corner blocks, a 1½" x 2" rectangle for tree trunk, and four 3" x 44" strips for outer ruffle.
4. From checked fabric, cut four 3½" x 12½" strips for borders, and two 16½" x 19" rectangles for pillow back.
5. Cut four red and three gold circles for the yo-yos.
6. From green print, cut four 1¼" x 9" bias strips for stems. From red print, cut four 2½" x 44" strips for inner ruffle.

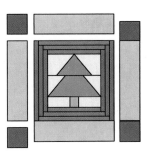

DIAGRAM F

DIAGRAM G

PIECING

1. Make tree block and add courthouse steps strips as instructed for the Quick-Sew Wallhanging Piecing Steps 1–4, pages 8 and 10.
2. Referring to Diagram F, add the checked border strips and brown print corner blocks.
3. Referring to the box on page 14, make seven yo-yos.
4. From green print fabric, trace and cut out five leaves. Press under ¼" around each leaf.
5. For the stems, fold each 1¼" bias strip in half lengthwise with wrong sides together, and press. Stitch a scant ¼" from the raw edges. Press the strip with the seam centered in back.
6. Referring to Diagram G, draw very light stem placement lines on the border. Position and pin the stems and leaves on the lines, tucking the leaves under the stems; slipstitch leaves and stems to pillow top.

7. Stitch the yo-yo flowers in place.

8. Refer to the General Instructions on page 7 to layer batting and muslin squares behind the pieced top. Quilt pillow top as desired.

9. Referring to Diagram H, make a mock double-ruffle using red and brown ruffle strips. Piece red inner ruffle strips together with diagonal seams. Piece brown outer ruffle strips together with diagonal seams. Sew red and brown strips together lengthwise.

10. Sew the short raw edges together with a diagonal seam forming a loop; trim the seam allowance to ¼". Referring to Diagram I, fold the loop in half lengthwise with wrong sides together; press. Sew a long gathering stitch ¼" from the raw edges.

11. Divide the ruffle into quarters and mark. Position the ruffle on the quilted pillow top with right sides together, raw edges even, and quarter marks on the corners. Pull the gathering thread so the ruffle fits the pillow top. Pin, and sew a scant ¼" from the raw edges.

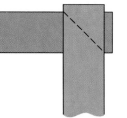

DIAGRAM H

12. Refer to Diagram J to make pillow back: Fold the two pillow back pieces in half with wrong sides together, forming two 9½" x 16½" double-thick pieces. Overlap the two folded edges by 2". Sew across the top and bottom, ¼" from the edge, to secure folds.

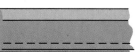

DIAGRAM I

13. Layer the back and pillow top with right sides together, and with the ruffle toward the center of the pillow; sew around the outside edges. Trim the corner seam allowances, if needed. Turn the pillow case right side out through the back opening and fluff the ruffle. Insert the pillow form.

DIAGRAM J

Pair of Mittens

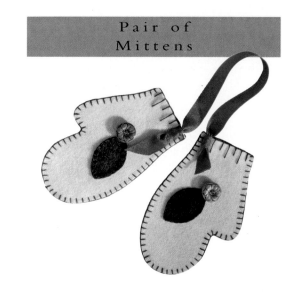

MATERIALS

- ¼ yard of white wool for mittens
- Scraps of green wool for leaves
- Fusible web
- Two ¾" gold or brass buttons
- Black embroidery floss
- 12" piece of ⅝"-wide brown grosgrain ribbon

CUTTING

1. Trace small mitten pattern from page 17. From white wool, cut four small mittens, reversing pattern for two if fabric is not reversible.

2. Refer to General Instructions on page 6 to trace, apply fusible web to, and cut two leaves from green wool.

ASSEMBLY AND FINISHING

1. Referring to the photograph above for placement, fuse leaves to two mittens.

2. Blanket-stitch around leaves with three strands of black embroidery floss. Sew button to mitten at bottom of each leaf.

3. Blanket-stitch a plain and an appliquéd mitten together with three strands of floss. Alternate long and short blanket stitches at the top edge of the mitten to simulate a cuff.

4. Tie a simple knot in the ends of the grosgrain ribbon and handsew one end to cuff of each mitten.

Mitten Garland

MATERIALS

- ¼ yard of white wool for mittens
- Scraps of green wool for leaves
- Fusible web
- Three ⅝" gold or brass buttons
- Green pearl cotton
- Black embroidery floss
- ⅛ yard of homespun check (60" wide fabric) for garland
- Scraps of red fabric for three yo-yos

DIAGRAM K

1. Trace large mitten and leaf patterns on page 17. From the white wool, cut six mitten shapes.

2. Refer to General Instructions on page 6 to trace, apply fusible web to, and cut six leaves from green wool.

3. Cut three red circles for yo-yos.

4. From homespun check, tear three 1" x 60" strips.

ASSEMBLY AND FINISHING

1. Referring to photograph for placement, fuse leaves to three of the mittens.

2. Blanket-stitch around leaves with three strands of black embroidery floss. Stem-stitch the stems with three strands of embroidery floss.

3. Referring to the box on page 14, make three yo-yo flowers; stitch to mittens. Tie the buttons to the yo-yos with pearl cotton thread.

4. Blanket-stitch together a plain and an appliquéd mitten with three strands of floss. Alternate long and short blanket stitches at the top edges of the mittens to simulate a cuff.

5. Sew homespun check strips together along the short edges. Referring to Diagram K, zigzag over a thread that is secured to the end of the strip. Gather strip to 26" long; knot thread ends.

6. Tie mittens to gathered strip with floss.

MATERIALS

- 4" x 5" piece of homespun check fabric
- Fusible web
- Scraps of red print fabric for three yo-yos
- Three ¾" buttons
- Scraps of green print fabric for leaves and stems
- Green pearl cotton thread
- 6" x 8" frame
- Heavy brown paper

A QUICK AND EASY YO-YO

After cutting out a circle, thread a needle with thread that matches the fabric. With the wrong side of the circle facing up, fold a ¼" seam allowance to the wrong side. Positioning knot in the seam allowance, stitch around the circle.

Pull the thread to gather the outside of the circle to the center, with the wrong side hidden inside the yo-yo. Pull until the circle is almost closed. Secure the thread with several small stitches.

Slightly flatten the yo-yo but do not press, since the gathers in the center become the center of the flower.

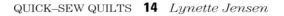

CUTTING

1. Trace one circle pattern from page 17. Cut three red circles for yo-yos.
2. Cut a 3" x 4" rectangle of fusible web.
3. Cut heavy paper to fit inside frame.
4. Refer to General Instructions on page 6 to trace, apply fusible web to, and cut a stem and two leaves from green print.

ASSEMBLY AND FINISHING

1. Fringe ¼" edges of homespun check rectangle; apply fusible web to back.
2. Make three yo-yos referring to the box, opposite. Tie buttons to yo-yos with pearl cotton thread.
3. Fuse homespun to paper. Referring to the photograph, fuse leaves and stem, and glue the yo-yos in place.
4. Insert completed piece into the frame.

Yo-Yo Flower Gift Bag

MATERIALS

- 5" x 7" piece of homespun check fabric
- Fusible web
- Small scraps of red print fabric for three yo-yos
- Scraps of green print fabric for leaves and stems
- Three ¾" buttons
- Green pearl cotton thread
- 8" x 12" brown paper bag with handles
- 1 yard of brown ⅝"-wide grosgrain ribbon

CUTTING

1. Trace circle pattern on page 17. Cut three red circles for yo-yos.
2. Cut a 4" x 6" rectangle of fusible web.
3. Refer to General Instructions on page 6 to trace, apply fusible web to, and cut a stem and two leaves from green print.

ASSEMBLY AND FINISHING

1. Fringe ¼" on all edges of the homespun check rectangle. Apply fusible web rectangle to homespun.
2. Make three yo-yos referring to the box, opposite. Tie buttons to yo-yos with pearl cotton thread.
3. Refer to the photograph for placement of homespun rectangle, leaves, stem, and yo-yos. Fuse homespun to bag. Fuse leaves and stem. Glue yo-yos in place.
4. Tie ribbon on handle.

Yo-Yo Flower
Note Card

MATERIALS

- 7" x 10" piece of heavy paper for card and a 5" x 7" heavy paper envelope
- 4" x 5" piece of homespun check fabric
- Fusible web
- Small scrap of red print fabric
- ¾" button
- Scraps of green print fabric for leaves and stems
- Green pearl cotton thread

ASSEMBLY AND FINISHING

1. Fringe ¼" on all sides of the homespun check rectangle. Apply fusible web rectangle to homespun.
2. Make one yo-yo flower, referring to the box on page 14. Tie button to yo-yo with pearl cotton.
3. Fold heavy paper in half to form card.
4. Referring to the photograph for placement, fuse homespun fabric to front of card. Fuse leaves and stem. Glue yo-yo flower in place.

CUTTING

1. Cut a 3" x 4" rectangle of fusible web.
2. Cut one red circle for yo-yo.
3. Refer to General Instructions on page 6 to trace, apply fusible web to, and cut a stem and two leaves from green print.

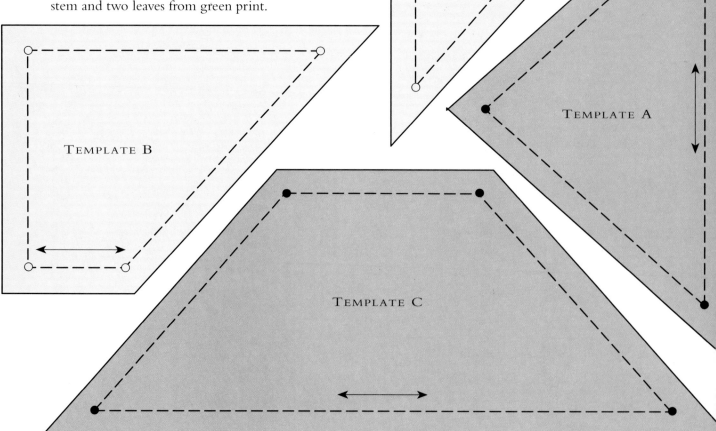

TEMPLATE D

TEMPLATE A

TEMPLATE B

TEMPLATE C

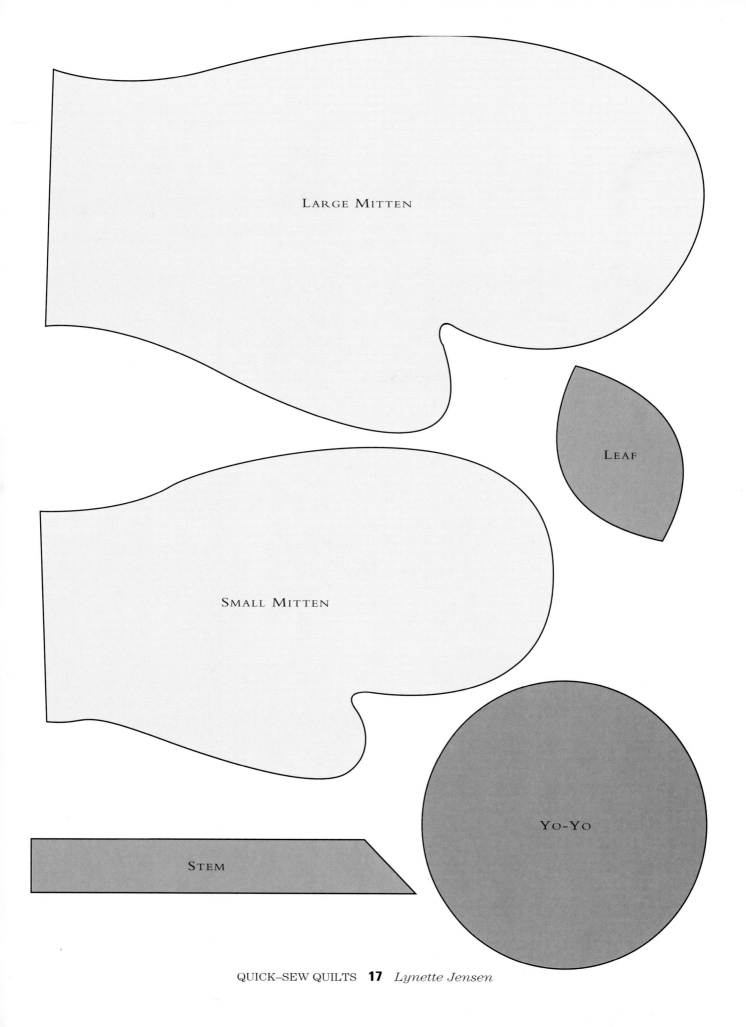

LARGE MITTEN

LEAF

SMALL MITTEN

YO-YO

STEM

Margaret Sindelar

BLUEBIRD OF HAPPINESS

Margaret Ann Sindelar's remarkable 25-year career as a needlework teacher, professional designer, and photo-stylist for book and magazine publishers is due in large part to her enduring admiration for the legendary Annie Oakley. After an aunt expanded Margaret's middle name to Annie, the Oakley soon followed to become a nickname that stuck.

And just what do a Wild-West "gunslinger" and a 20th century woman with a Master's Degree in Family Economics and Management have in common? Margaret's research reveals interesting parallels in their lives. While Oakley's sewing skills were learned in an orphanage and Margaret's were developed through a college curriculum, both developed a lifelong love of the needlearts.

For shooting competitions Annie always wore a lucky-star badge. While on the road with her Wild West show, Oakley designed and made the elaborate beaded and fringed show costumes and filled her trunk with embroidery and fancy needlework.

Margaret Sindelar has followed Annie Oakley's footsteps to create similar works of enduring art, through her design company—Cottonwood Classics—and by wearing her own lucky star badge!

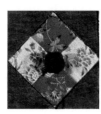

MATERIALS

- ½ yard of muslin for background
- 1 yard of burgundy print fabric for backing, border, flower centers, and corner blocks
- ¼ yard each of yellow and rust print fabrics for border blocks
- ½ yard each of blue-on-blue print fabrics for border triangles and bird appliqué
- ⅛ yard each of blue and green print fabrics for flower appliqué
- Large scraps of rust, red, and green print fabrics for appliqué
- 1 yard of multicolor stripe fabric for wide binding
- Four 4mm black beads
- Eighteen ¾" rust buttons
- Fusible web
- Batting
- Blue, rust, pink, green, yellow, red, brown, dark gray, dark red, and orange embroidery floss

Quick-Sew Wallhanging

Finished size 27" x 30"

CUTTING

1. From the muslin, cut a 16½" x 20½"rectangle.
2. From burgundy print, cut two 1¼" x 44" crosswise strips, and four 4½" squares.
3. From the yellow and rust prints, cut thirty-six 1⅞" A squares.
4. From blue-on-blue print, cut seven 5¼" squares. Cut squares in half diagonally in both directions, making 28 B triangles. Cut eight 2⅞" squares; cut in half diagonally, making 16 C triangles.
5. Refer to General Instructions on page 6 to trace, apply fusible web to, and cut these appliqués on page 26: From burgundy print, cut five flower centers. From blue print fabric, cut five flowers. From green print fabric, cut ten leaves. From the blue-on-blue print, cut two birds in one direction and reverse the pattern for two birds in the other direction. Repeat for the bird wings in rust print.
6. Cut four 4½" x 36" strips for binding.

APPLIQUÉ

1. Referring to the photograph and the directions that follow, fuse appliqué pieces to the muslin; machine- or hand-appliqué as directed. Refer to the Stitch Guide on page 29 for appliqué-stitch ideas.

2. Position the five sets of flower leaves ½" above the bottom edge of the muslin and evenly spaced. Angle them out so they are 2½" across; fuse. Position the flower with the center tucked slightly under the dip. Fuse, and blanket-stitch around all pieces. Stem-stitch the stems with green floss. Using long stitches and French knots, embroider the three stamens with yellow floss.

3. Position the bluebirds so their heads are ½" from the top edge of the muslin, and spaced about ¾" apart; fuse. Position wing on each bird; fuse. Blanket-stitch around all pieces. With orange floss, stem-stitch and long-stitch the feet, and satin-stitch the beaks.

4. Lightly draw five lines across the muslin as a base for the letters and numbers, drawing the first one ¾" above the flower row and marking the others 2½" apart.

5. Lightly mark the letters and numbers on the lines. Stem-stitch the letters with three strands of dark gray floss, and numbers with dark red floss.

PIECING

1. Fold each burgundy strip in half lengthwise with wrong sides together; press. With right sides together and raw edges matching, sew a folded strip to top edge of muslin; cut excess strip, and repeat on the bottom edge. Do not press

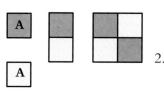

DIAGRAM A

DIAGRAM B

the strips away from the center. Sew the remaining folded strips to the side edges of the muslin.

2. Referring to Diagram A, piece the yellow and rust A squares together, forming 18 checkerboard blocks.

3. Referring to Diagram B and using the B and C blue-on-blue triangles, sew two strips each with four checkerboard blocks, and two strips each with five checkerboard blocks.

4. Sew long strips to side edges of the muslin; press open. Sew the burgundy squares to the ends of shorter strips; sew strips to top and bottom edges of muslin (Diagram C).

5. Referring to the photograph, cut, fuse and appliqué the cherries and cherry leaves in the burgundy squares. Blanket-stitch around cherries and leaves with three strands of red and green floss. Add brown stems using a stem stitch.

FINISHING

1. Cut a 32" x 44" rectangle each from the backing fabric and the batting.

2. Refer to General Instructions on page 7 to layer wallhanging.

3. Trim the batting and backing, leaving a 1¾" margin beyond edges of the pieced top. Sew around, ¼" from outside edges.

4. With right sides together and raw edges matching, sew a binding strip to one edge of top, beginning and ending ¼" inside edges with a back stitch (Diagram D). Sew remaining strips to top, being careful not to catch strips in the seams.

5. Press the binding strips away from the center, overlapping ends to make square intersections (Diagram E).

DIAGRAM C

6. Press under one end of the top strip at a 45° angle (Diagram F). Machine- or hand-sew the angled corner seam. Trim excess fabric.

7. Turn binding fabric to the back, press under ¼" and stitch to backing.

8. Sew a black bead at the X on each bluebird for eye, and a rust button in the center of each pieced diamond.

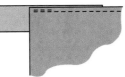

DIAGRAM D

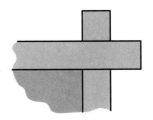

DIAGRAM E

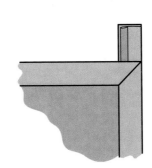

diagram F

Folk Art Jacket

MATERIALS

- Jacket pattern
- Red print fabric in yardage specified on pattern
- ½ yard each of aqua, brown, medium blue, and rust print fabrics for pieced stripes
- ½ yard each of periwinkle, wine, and mocha fabrics for appliqué strips
- ¼ yard each of green, light rust, mustard, mauve, turquoise, and fuchsia solid fabrics for narrow stripes
- ⅛ yard each of two blues, two greens, dark mauve, rust, and red print fabrics for appliqué
- ¼ yard of beige print fabric for pieced stripe
- Fusible web
- 1 yard of multicolor print fabric
- Lightweight batting
- 5 yards of narrow sew-in black piping
- Twenty 4mm black beads for eyes
- Twenty-six 1" red buttons
- Blue, green, brown, and red thread
- Green, yellow, orange, and brown embroidery floss

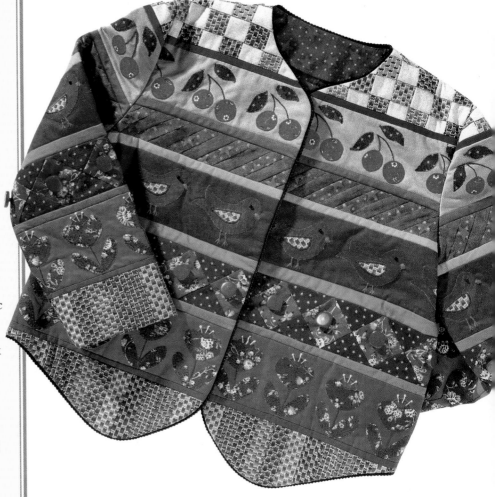

CUTTING AND MARKING

1. Cut all jacket pattern pieces from red print fabric, including facings.

2. With wrong sides together, sew the side seams using a ⅝" seam allowance; press seam allowances open.

3. Lay the jacket body on a flat surface, wrong side up. Lay the sleeves next to the jacket, wrong side up, with the armhole notches on the same level.

4. Referring to Diagram G, use tailor's chalk or quilter's marking pencil to draw a line about 1½" above the highest point of the bottom edge of the jacket (on our pattern it is the back). This is the baseline for the periwinkle strip.

5. Cut the following strips in the widths indicated and in a length that is the width of the jacket body plus the width of both sleeves. For most sizes, two 44" strips should be enough.

6. For appliqué strips, cut 4½" periwinkle, 4" wine, and 3¾" mocha strips.

7. For solid strips, cut 1" green, light rust, mustard, mauve, and turquoise strips and 1¼" fuchsia strips.

8. For the diamond pieced strip, cut two 2½" strips from rust print and four 2½" strips from the medium blue print.

9. For diagonal pieced strip, cut six 1½" strips of aqua and brown.

10. For the checkerboard shoulder area, cut four 1¾" strips from beige print and four 1¾" strips from multicolor print.

11. For the bottom strip, cut multicolor fabric wide enough to cover from the baseline to about 1" below the bottom edge of the jacket.

12. Refer to the General Instructions on page 6 to trace, apply fusible web to, and cut the following appliqué pieces on page 26: Cut 26 each blue print flowers and dark mauve print flower centers,

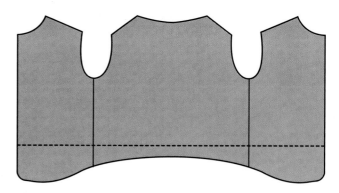

DIAGRAM G

and 52 green print flower leaves for the periwinkle strip; cut 22 each blue print bluebirds and rust print wings for the wine strip; cut 28 each red print cherries and green print cherry leaves for the mocha strip.

APPLIQUÉ AND PIECING

1. Fuse and then machine-appliqué the pieces to the strips referring to the photograph and the directions below. Machine-appliqué at the step directed. Refer to the Stitch Guide on page 29 for machine-appliqué stitch ideas.

2. Position two flower leaves above the bottom edge of the periwinkle strips with the two points overlapping slightly and angled so they are 2½" across. Arrange each next set of angled leaves about ½" apart; fuse. Position each flower with the center tucked slightly under the dip; fuse and appliqué around pieces. Embroider stems using a stem stitch and green floss, and three stamens using a long stitch and a French knot and yellow floss.

3. Position the bluebirds so their bellies are 1" from the bottom of the wine strips, and spaced about ½" apart; fuse. Position a wing on each bird and fuse. With orange embroidery floss, use stem and long-stitches for feet, and satin-stitch a beak on each bird.

4. Position cherries and leaves on the mocha strips, allowing for the cherry stems and leaving about ½" between bunches; fuse. With brown embroidery floss, stem-stitch stems.

5. For the pieced diamond strip, sew a rust strip in between the medium blue print strips. Cut the piece crosswise at right angles into 2½" strips. Referring to Diagram H, sew the strips together, matching the top edge of one rust square with the bottom edge of the next square. Make two strips. Trim long edges of the pieced strips ¼" above and below the rust diamond (Diagram I).

6. For the diagonal pieced strip, sew an aqua and brown strip together along long edges; add the remaining strips, alternating colors. Cut the piece crosswise at 45° angles into 2½" strips. Referring to Diagram J, join the strips together continuing alternating colors.

7. For the checkerboard strip, sew a beige print strip and a multicolored strip together along long edges; add the remaining strips, alternating colors. Cut the piece crosswise at right angles into 1¾" strips. Referring to Diagram K, sew strips together, alternating colors to form a checkerboard pattern.

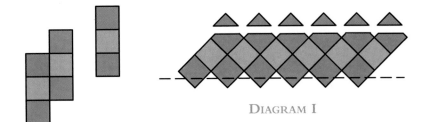

DIAGRAM I

DIAGRAM H

DIAGRAM J

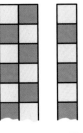

DIAGRAM K

SEWING AND QUILTING

1. Lay the red print jacket body and sleeves right side up on batting; baste. Cut batting about 2" larger than red fabric. With the yardstick as a guide, mark the baseline from the red print to the batting on all three pieces.

2. Working directly on the batting, strip-piece the jacket body and sleeves according to the directions below, sewing the prepared strips on the body first, then on the two sleeves.

3. Position the bottom edge of the appliquéd flower strip on the baseline mark with whole flowers near the front edges. Cut strips at batting edges. Lay the green strip over the bottom edge of the flower strip with right sides together and raw edges matching. Sew ¼" from the edges. Press green strip down.

4. Lay the light rust strip along the top edge of the flower strip; stitch (Diagram L) and press up.

5. Continue adding strips in the following order, keeping the long edges even and pressing before adding the next strip: pieced diamond, fuchsia, appliquéd bluebird, mustard, diagonal pieced, mauve, appliquéd cherries, turquoise and finally, the checkerboard. If necessary, add checkerboard pieces to the shoulder area for height.

6. Return to the bottom. Add the multicolor print to the green strip and press down.

7. Staystitch ¼" inside all the edges of the jacket pieces. Trim away the excess batting and strips.

8. Assemble jacket according to pattern directions, inserting black piping in the seams of the jacket opening.

9. Sew a black bead at the X on each bluebird as an eye and a red button in the center of each pieced diamond.

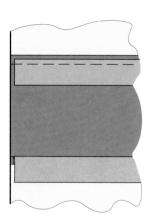

DIAGRAM L

CHERRY NAPKIN

For each napkin, cut one 18" square of beige fabric. Trace, apply fusible web to, and cut out two cherries and two leaves. Fuse and appliqué the cherries and the leaves about 1½" from one corner. Blanket-stitch around the appliqués with red and green embroidery floss. Add brown stems using a stem stitch. Machine-sew with matching thread around the napkin about ¾" in from the edges. Fringe the edges.

MINI TOTE

Use your favorite pouch-type purse pattern to make the bag from artificial suede and the flap from crazy-quilt patchwork. Decorate the bag with metallic threads, and embellish the crazy-quilting with an embroidered bluebird, flower, and cherries from the patterns on page 26.

Bird Trio Bell Pull

14" long

MATERIALS

- 4" x 12" piece each of lavender, aqua, and brown artificial suede
- Scrap of three different coordinating print fabrics for wings
- Scrap of red/orange fabric for beak
- Polyester stuffing
- Three 4mm black beads
- Coordinating thread
- Brown pearl cotton thread
- Eight novelty glass beads
- 1½" bell

CUTTING

1. Trace and cut out two large birds from each color. If you are not using artificial suede, reverse the patterns.
2. Refer to the General Instructions on page 6 to trace, apply fusible web to, and cut out two large wings for each bird.
3. Trace and cut three beaks.
4. Cut two 36" lengths of pearl cotton thread.

SEWING

1. Fuse the coordinating wings to the birds, using a press cloth to protect the suede; zigzag with coordinating thread.
2. With wrong sides together, zigzag-stitch the two bird pieces together using matching thread, leaving a small opening for stuffing.
3. Stuff with polyester stuffing. Stitch opening closed.
4. Sew a beak and a black bead for an eye on each bird.
5. Fold pearl cotton thread in half and tie a knot about 3" from the fold. Thread the pearl cotton thread through two beads and the center of a bird three times. Thread through the last two beads and the bell and then tie off.

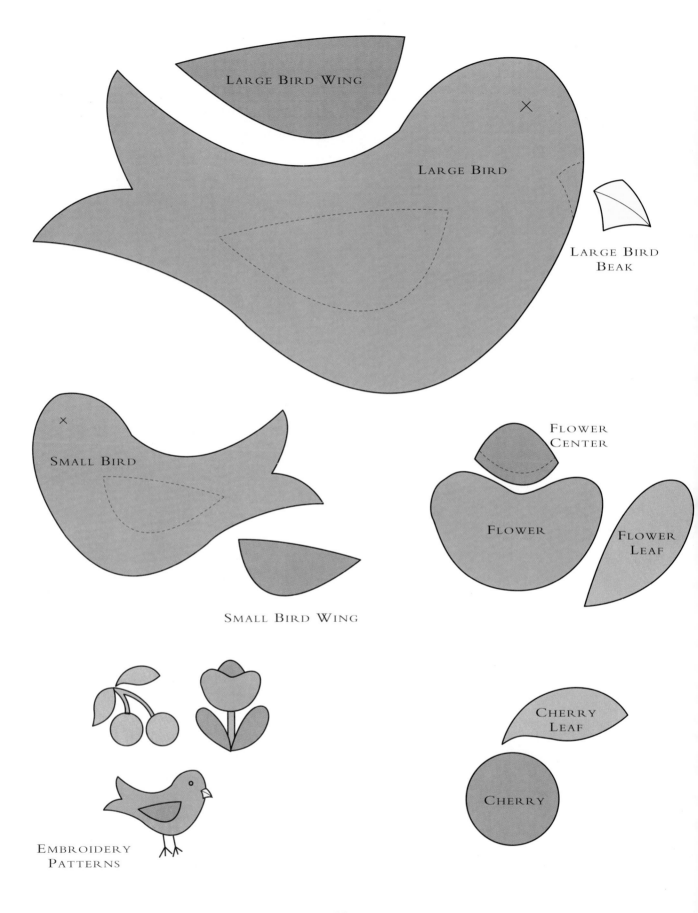

LARGE BIRD WING

LARGE BIRD

LARGE BIRD
BEAK

SMALL BIRD

SMALL BIRD WING

FLOWER
CENTER

FLOWER

FLOWER
LEAF

CHERRY
LEAF

CHERRY

EMBROIDERY
PATTERNS

1234567890

ABCDEFGHIJK

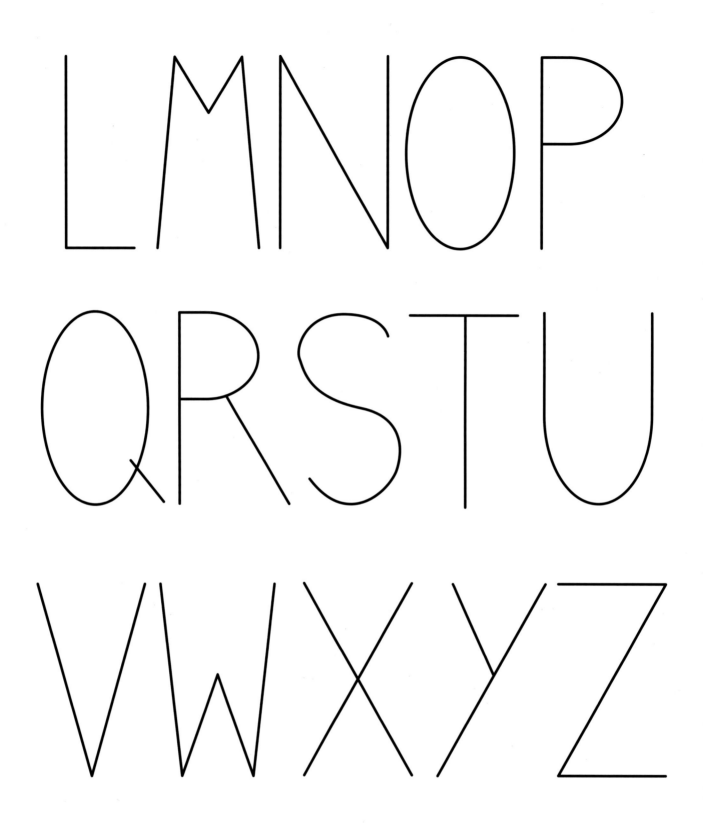

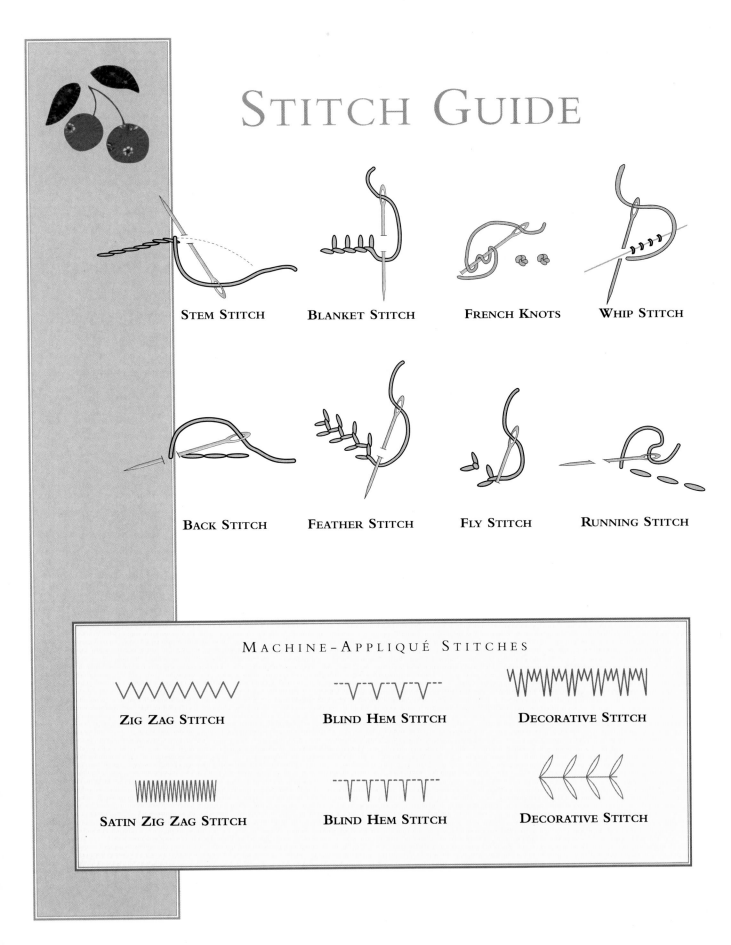

STITCH GUIDE

STEM STITCH   **BLANKET STITCH**   **FRENCH KNOTS**   **WHIP STITCH**

BACK STITCH   **FEATHER STITCH**   **FLY STITCH**   **RUNNING STITCH**

MACHINE-APPLIQUÉ STITCHES

ZIG ZAG STITCH   **BLIND HEM STITCH**   **DECORATIVE STITCH**

SATIN ZIG ZAG STITCH   **BLIND HEM STITCH**   **DECORATIVE STITCH**

Sandy Belt

Life's a zoo—literally, for folk art designer Sandy Belt, whose enchanting one-of-a-kind animal creations have been exhibited in numerous collections from FolkWorks Gallery in Evanston, Illinois, to The Museum of American Folk Art in New York City.

Fortunately, Sandy's cloth creations require much less care than her family of nine. But her large, close-knit family became the impetus for Sandy's surprising career. Raising seven children in a farmhouse near Marquette, Michigan, Sandy and her husband, Tom, a fireman, were struggling to make ends meet. To save money, Sandy taught herself to sew and made all the kids' clothes. A mid-life crisis and help from art appreciators launched her career.

"When my mother died of breast cancer and my oldest daughter moved away from home, I felt life was short and I needed to do something to express myself," Sandy recalls. Sandy began fashioning award-winning dolls and then expanded upon her designs to create fashions, vests, bags, and home decor items for national publications and a major pattern company. Sandy is also largely responsible for bringing folk art colors into felt—a wonderful medium for her fanciful work.

As a special treat, try a sampling of Sandy Belt's animal pairs on felt or fabric.

MATERIALS

- 1 yard of black felt for background
- 1 yard of gold felt for backing
- 1 yard of denim felt for border
- Two 12" squares each of antique white, cinnamon, and light tan felt for appliqué
- One 12" square each of gray, walnut, and mustard felt for appliqué
- 4 skeins of black pearl cotton thread

Quick–Sew Wallhanging

Finished size 25" x 34"

CUTTING

1. From the black, gold and denim blue felt, cut 25" x 34" rectangles.
2. Using pattern on page 37, cut a corner template from heavy paper. Referring to Diagram A, place the template on one corner of the black background rectangle. Cut along the rounded side of the template. Repeat for the remaining corners. Using the same method, round the corners of the gold backing and denim blue border rectangles.
3. Using pattern on pages 42–43, and referring to Diagram B, cut a sawtooth center template from heavy paper.

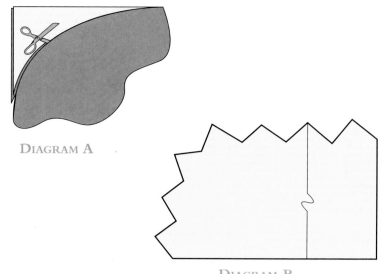

DIAGRAM A

DIAGRAM B

4. Referring to Diagram C, fold the denim blue felt in half in each direction. Place the border template on the felt, matching the bottom right corners. Cut the felt following the sawtooth edge of the template.

5. Referring to the General Instructions on page 6, trace and cut out the following appliqué pieces on pages 37–41: Two each swan, dog, and goose; one each cat, giraffe, dove, moon, deer with antlers and deer without antlers; the respective animal spots, ears, tail sections and beaks; a full set of ark pieces (bottom, deck, wave, cabin, roof and windows); five stars; two each of T, W, and O, and one X.

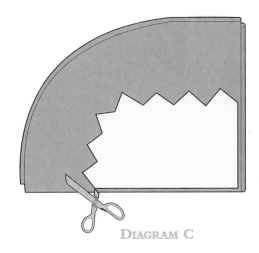

DIAGRAM C

ASSEMBLY

1. Referring to the photograph and the directions below, apply appliqué pieces to black background and denim blue border, layering as indicated by dashed lines on the pattern pieces. Use black pearl cotton thread for appliqué stitches.

2. Blanket-stitch the wave to the ark deck and the circles to the ark cabin.

3. Center the ark bottom about 5" from the bottom edge of the black background. Blanket-stitch all ark pieces to black background, including the giraffe (Diagram D).

4. Attach giraffe horns with running stitches (Diagram E).

5. Center the denim blue border over the black background. Blanket-stitch the sawtooth edge.

6. Blanket-stitch most appliqué pieces in place as shown in photograph. Use a running stitch to attach white spots on the goose, dog spots and ears, swan beaks and the stars. Add whiskers with a long stitch and eyes with a half feather stitch (Diagram F).

DIAGRAM D

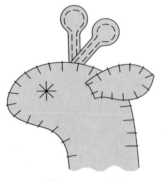

DIAGRAM E

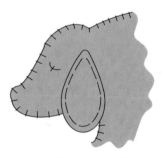

DIAGRAM F

FINISHING

1. Center black and denim blue appliquéd piece over gold backing. Use black pearl cotton thread to feather-stitch the edge through all layers.

BEST FRIENDS PILLOW

Your favorite animals from the menagerie featured on the ark wallhanging can be forever friends on a charming 7" x 10" mini-pillow like the one shown here. Have fun adding your own imaginative embellishments!

Kid's Felt Vest

MATERIALS

- 1 yard of denim felt for vest and lining
- 12" square of light tan felt for deer
- Scraps of mustard and antique white felt for stars and moon
- 2 skeins black pearl cotton
- 35 assorted sizes white buttons
- Kid's felt vest pattern or any vest pattern without darts

CUTTING

1. From the denim felt, cut two sets of the vest fronts and two vest backs (one set is for the lining).
2. Refer to the General Instructions on page 6 to trace and cut out the following appliqué pieces on page 43: Small deer with antlers, small deer without antlers, two deer ears, two tails, four small stars and one small moon.

ASSEMBLY AND FINISHING

1. Referring to the photograph and the directions below, apply appliqué pieces to one set of vest fronts, layering as indicated by dashed lines on the pattern pieces.
2. With black pearl cotton thread, blanket-stitch around the deer and moon and use running stitches to apply the stars.
3. Sew vest fronts to vest back at shoulder and side seams. Repeat for vest lining.
4. Place the vest and lining for vest together with right sides out. Using black pearl cotton thread, blanket-stitch around the edges.
5. Sew a button in the center of each star. Sew several buttons near the right front edge and as a wide "V" on the left shoulder.

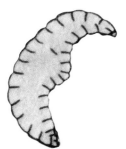

Makes two 18" tall cats

MATERIALS

- ¼ yard of muslin for cat heads, body fronts, and paws
- Large scraps of dark gray and floral print fabric for backs and front legs
- Large scraps of striped and brown fabric for hind legs
- Scraps of print and plaid fabric for crazy-quilt fronts
- Polyester filling
- Antique white, gray, and black paint
- Black and gray pearl cotton thread
- Gold embroidery floss
- Black permanent fabric pen
- Assorted white and colored buttons, ribbon, and lace for embellishment

HEADS

1. Trace and cut out pattern on page 44. Cut four heads from muslin.

2. On the right side of two heads, trace facial features with a pencil, marking one with a keyhole-shaped painting line for the black cat.

3. With right sides together, sew around head, leaving bottom open; turn right side out. Hand-sew across base of ears with a small running stitch. Stuff head and neck firmly.

4. Paint entire calico cat head with antique white paint. Let dry. To paint stripes on cat's face, dip corner of foam brush in gray paint. Make quick short strokes from center of face toward a seam. Add a few stripes to back of head. Let dry.

5. To paint the black cat's face, dampen a foam brush with water; squeeze tight. Apply black paint to brush. Paint back of head and face, leaving the keyhole-shaped area unpainted. Make sure paint covers seams; sometimes it takes two coats. Let dry.

6. Draw facial features with permanent pen. Refer to Diagram G to run a double strand of pearl cotton thread through each set of dots for the cat's whiskers.

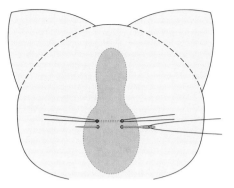

DIAGRAM G

BODIES

1. Trace and cut out body pattern on page 45. Cut two body pieces from muslin and one each from the back fabrics.

2. Referring to Diagram H, cut a scrap of fabric with 4 or 5 edges. Place in center of one body piece. With right sides together, place a second scrap on top of first one aligning one edge; sew with a ¼" seam allowance. Open out the top fabric and press. Trim ¼" larger all around than desired size. Repeat with additional scraps until body piece is covered. Trim scrap edges even with muslin.

3. Referring to Diagrams I and J and Stitch Guide on page 29 for stitch ideas, use three strands of gold floss to embroider the seams.

4. With right sides together, sew front to back along the sides, leaving the neck open between dots and leaving the bottom open. Insert the head into the body through the neck opening, stopping at the dotted line on the neck; hand-sew in place. Stuff body to within 1" of bottom, making sure long end of neck is centered in body.

5. Fold in bottom edges as if wrapping a gift: sides first, then back, then front. Turn under raw front edge; sew.

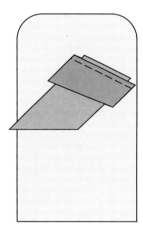
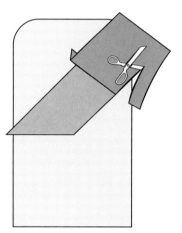

DIAGRAM H

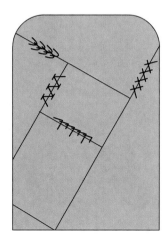
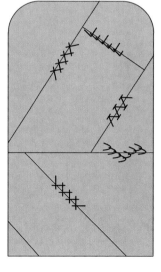

CALICO CAT - DIAGRAM I   BLACK CAT - DIAGRAM J

FRONT LEGS

1. Trace and cut out pattern on page 45. For each set of front legs, cut one 1½" x 7" strip of muslin for paws and one 7" x 8" rectangle of print fabric for legs; sew the pieces together along the 7" edges. Referring to Diagram K, cut four legs, placing dashed pattern line on seam between muslin and print fabric.

2. Place two leg pieces with right sides together; sew all around, leaving top open. Turn right side out. Repeat for other leg. Paint paws antique white. Stuff legs to dotted line on pattern. Turn in raw edges ¼"; sew legs to body near neck.

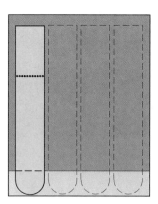

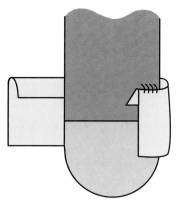

DIAGRAM K   DIAGRAM L

HIND LEGS

1. Trace and cut out pattern on page 44. For each cat, cut four hind leg pieces from desired fabric. Place two legs with right sides together; sew all around, leaving top open. Turn right side out. Stuff legs to dotted line on pattern. Turn in raw edges ¼"; sew legs to lower edge of body back.

FINISHING

1. Tea stain all body parts, referring to Tips & Techniques on page 83.

2. Referring to the photographs and the directions below, embellish the cats.

3. Sew the buttons or charms to the crazy-quilted body.

4. For lace collar, cut a 6" piece of ribbon, and an 8" piece of lace. Starting in center of lace, thread ribbon through top edge of lace with a large-eyed needle. Place around cat's neck; pull ribbon tight, gathering the lace. Tie ribbon in a bow, trim ends.

5. For lace cuffs, sew strips of lace around wrists, covering seam.

6. For high collar, trace and cut out pattern on page 44. Cut one collar from muslin. Fold in half with right sides together and sew short seams. Turn right side out and press. Overcast raw neck edges; press to wrong side. Place the collar around the cat's neck. Secure with a button at center front.

7. For cuffs, cut one 1¼" x 6" piece of muslin. Fold piece in half lengthwise with right sides together and sew short seams. Turn right side out; press under long raw edge. Cut strip in half crosswise. Referring to Diagram L, handsew each half around a wrist, overlapping the cuff's cut edge with the finished edge and covering the wrist seam.

8. Apply powder blush to cheeks.

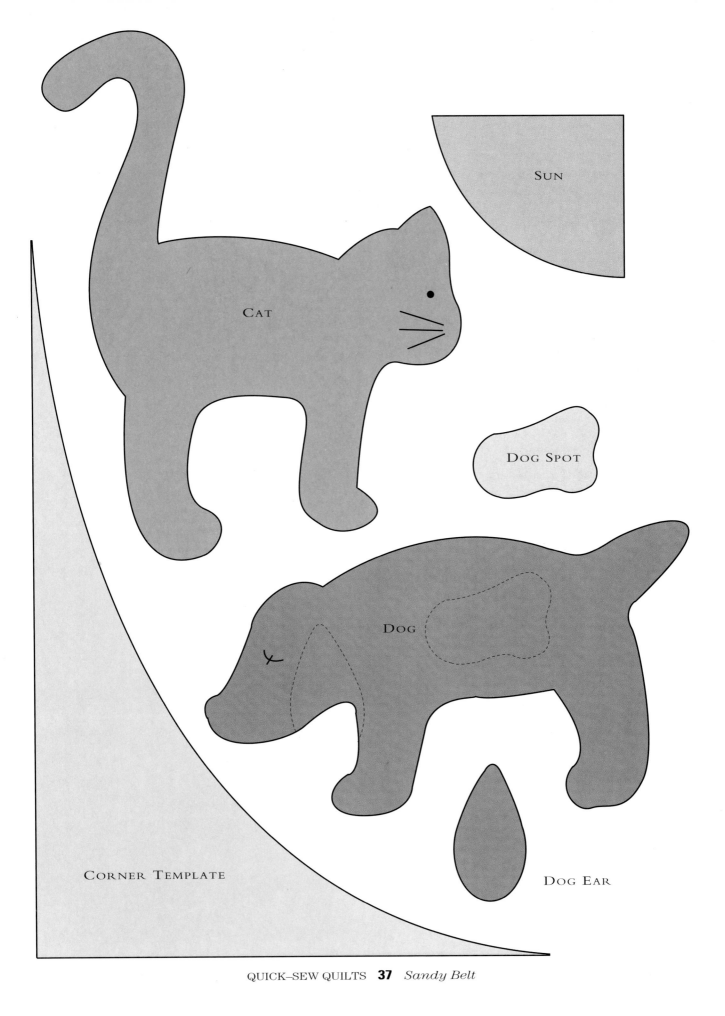

SUN

CAT

DOG SPOT

DOG

CORNER TEMPLATE

DOG EAR

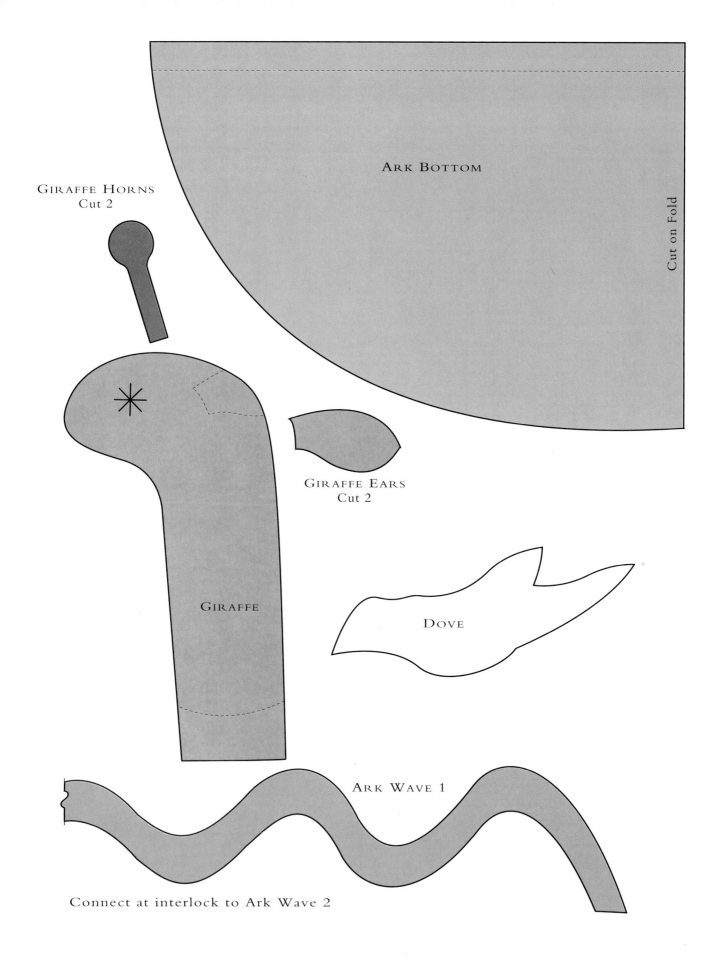

ARK BOTTOM

Cut on Fold

GIRAFFE HORNS
Cut 2

GIRAFFE EARS
Cut 2

GIRAFFE

DOVE

ARK WAVE 1

Connect at interlock to Ark Wave 2

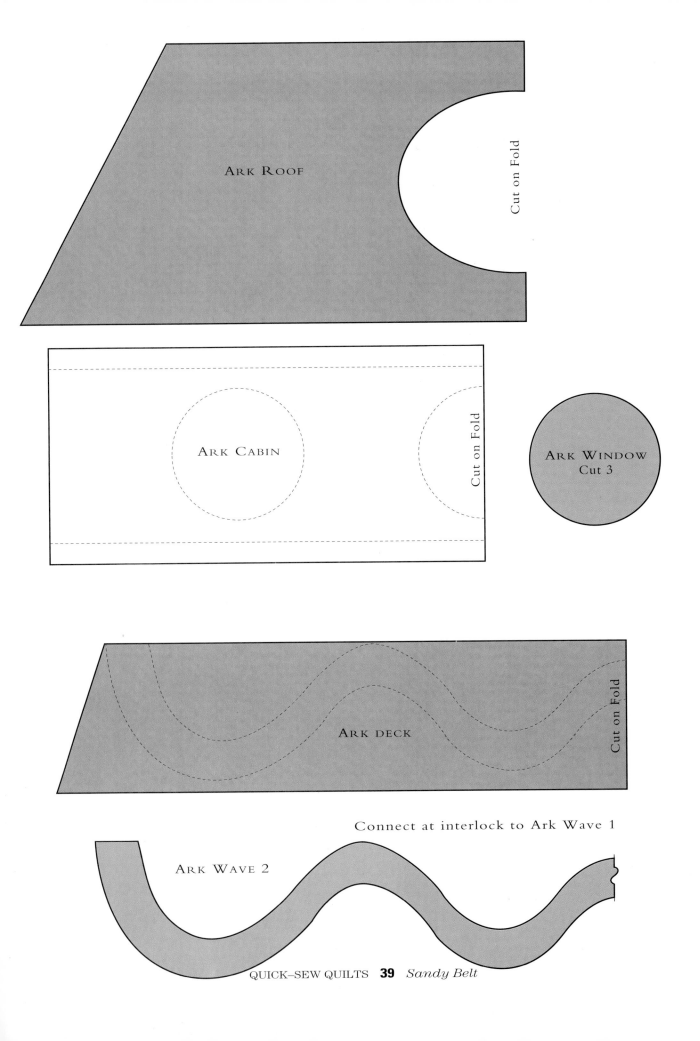

ARK ROOF

Cut on Fold

ARK CABIN

Cut on Fold

ARK WINDOW
Cut 3

ARK DECK

Cut on Fold

Connect at interlock to Ark Wave 1

ARK WAVE 2

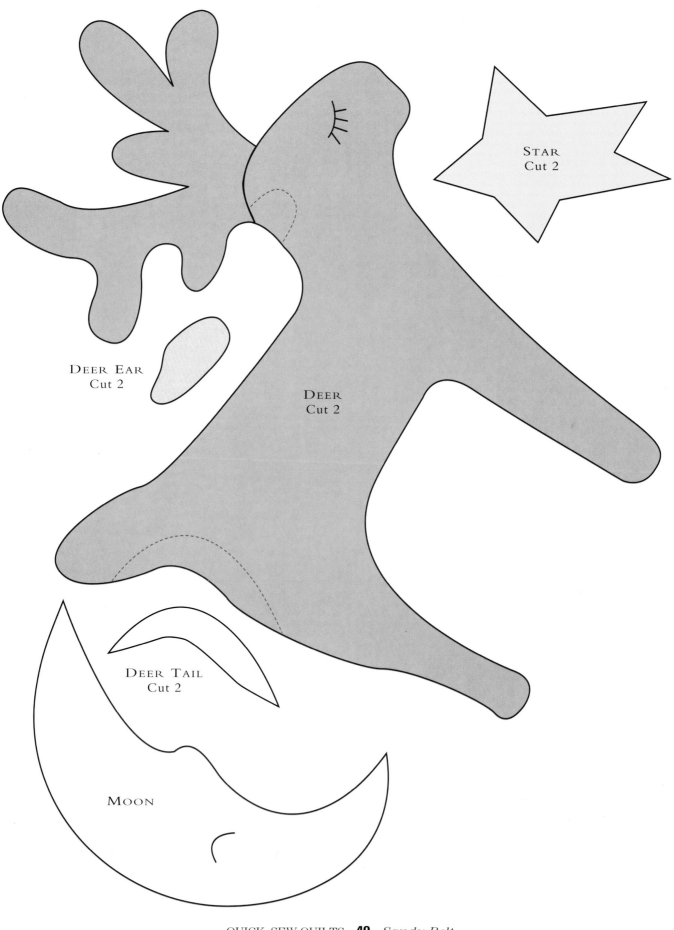

STAR
Cut 2

DEER EAR
Cut 2

DEER
Cut 2

DEER TAIL
Cut 2

MOON

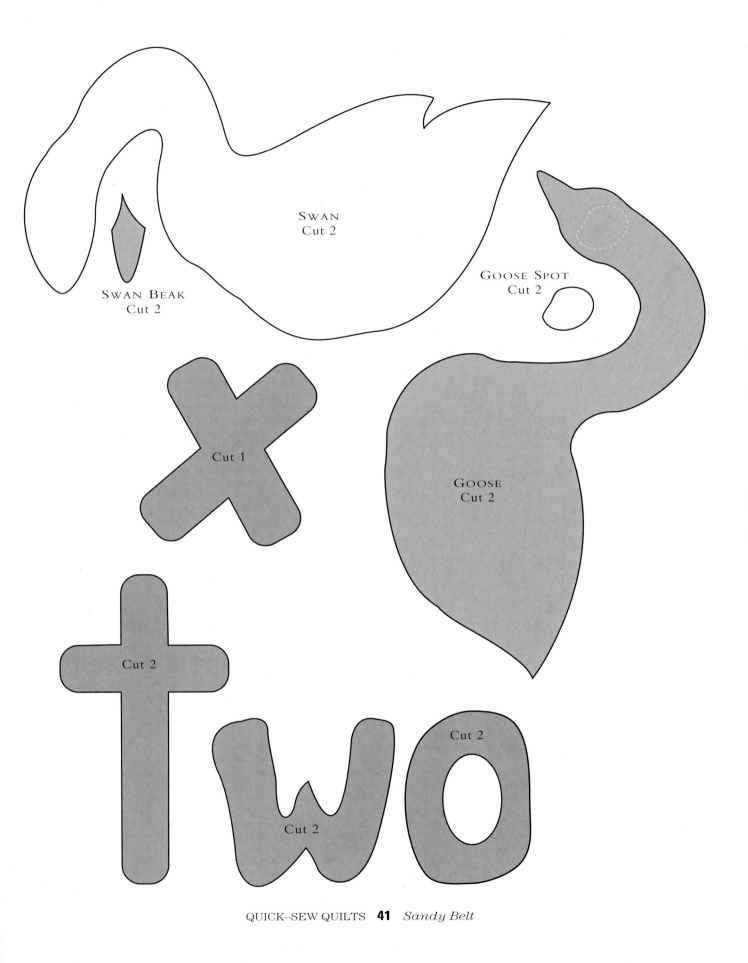

SWAN
Cut 2

SWAN BEAK
Cut 2

GOOSE SPOT
Cut 2

GOOSE
Cut 2

Cut 1

Cut 2

Cut 2

Cut 2

Cut 2

Sawtooth Center 1

Connect at interlock to Sawtooth Center 2

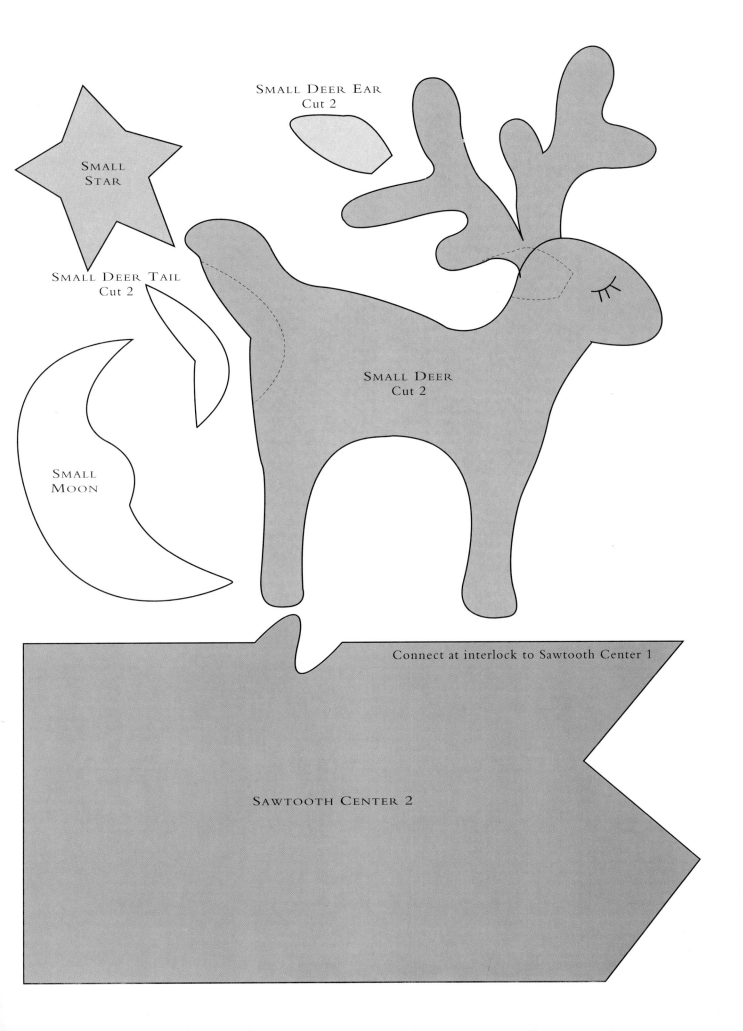

SMALL DEER EAR
Cut 2

SMALL
STAR

SMALL DEER TAIL
Cut 2

SMALL
MOON

SMALL DEER
Cut 2

Connect at interlock to Sawtooth Center 1

SAWTOOTH CENTER 2

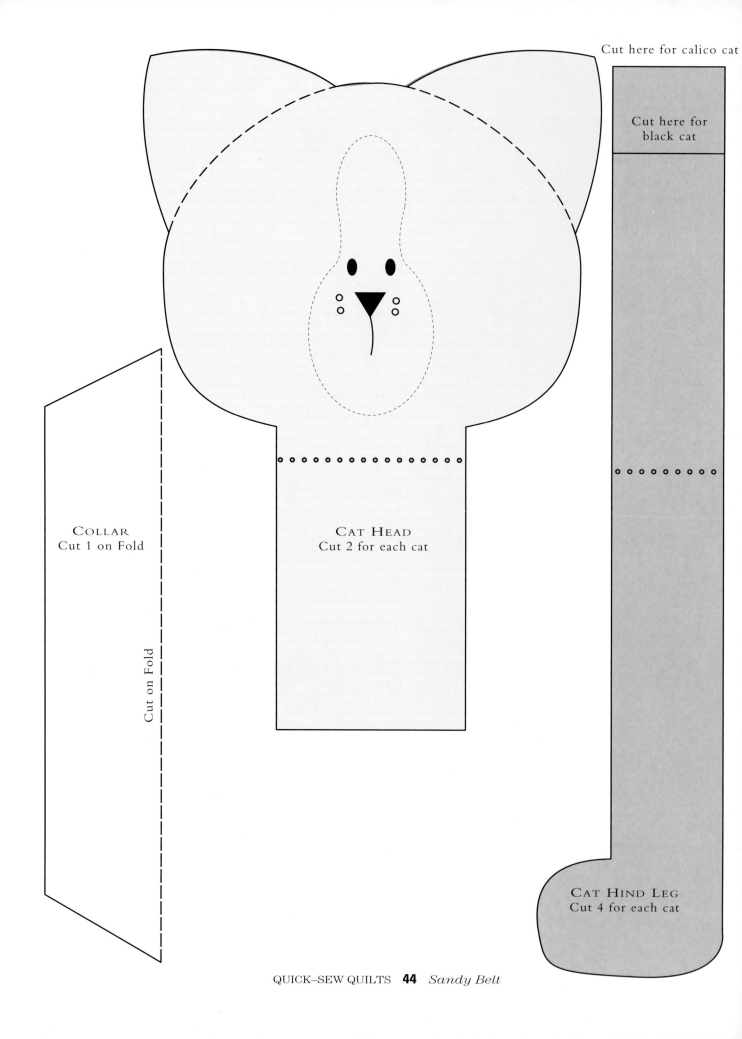

Cut here for calico cat

Cut here for
black cat

COLLAR
Cut 1 on Fold

Cut on Fold

CAT HEAD
Cut 2 for each cat

CAT HIND LEG
Cut 4 for each cat

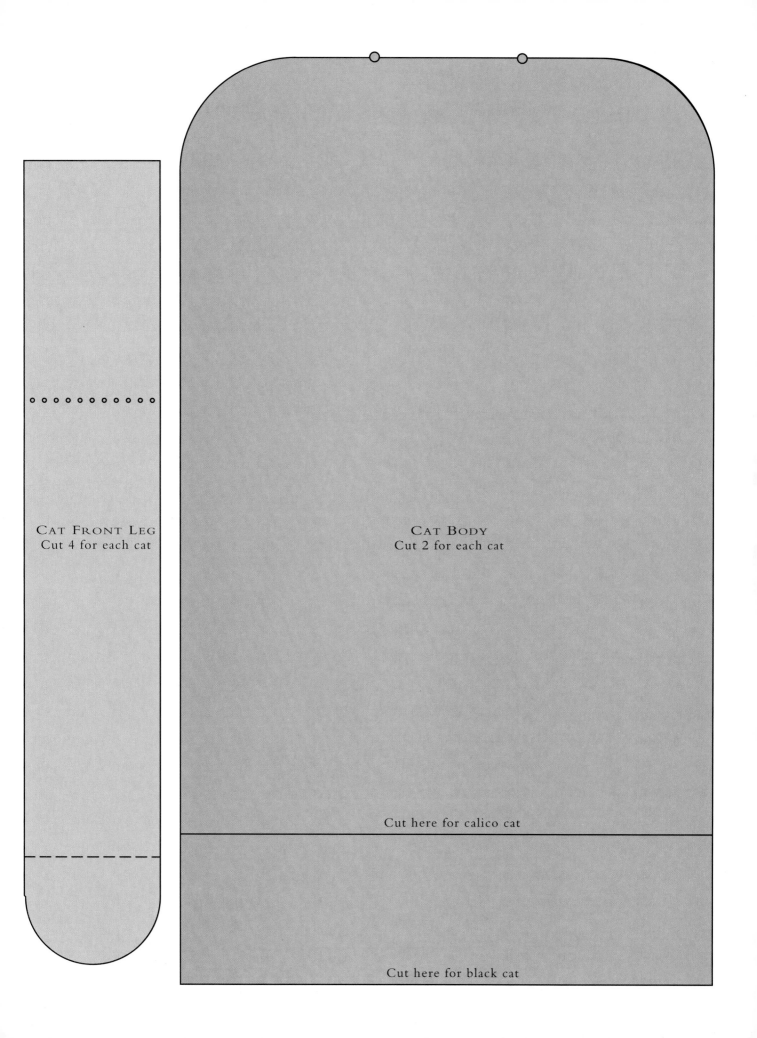

CAT FRONT LEG
Cut 4 for each cat

CAT BODY
Cut 2 for each cat

Cut here for calico cat

Cut here for black cat

Sally Korte and Alice Strebel

When Sally Korte and Alice Strebel met through a mutual friend, starting a business was the last thing on their minds. Since they both wanted to dress differently, they decided to go shopping together. Still not finding anything, Sally and Alice began designing clothing for themselves with a unique primitive look. Admiring friends clamored for the handmade fashions; when it became too much work, their friends suggested, "If you had patterns, we could make it ourselves."

From that unlikely beginning, their business—Kindred Spirits—came into being. Although Kindred Spirits has grown in the past nine years to include four books and 30 patterns, gaining them national recognition and a loyal following, their design philosophy remains unchanged.

According to Sally, "Our goal is to be an inspiration to those in the needlework arts who want to 1. Have fun. 2. Start with something simple and add 'stuff' to make it unique. 3. Take what they start...change it...finish it to please themselves." And the business itself has been an inspiration to Sally and Alice whose emphasis is a shared faith—best expressed in their signature phrase—"May all the creations of our hands be clear reflections of the Creator."

MATERIALS

- ¾ yard of black wool fabric for background and backing
- Large scraps of cream, gold, red, brown, and blue wool; and green boiled wool for patches and appliqué
- Black thread
- Black wool thread

Quick–Sew Wallhanging

Finished size 15" x 26"

CUTTING

1. From black wool background and backing fabric, cut two 16" x 27" rectangles.
2. From cream wool, cut a 6" x 16" rectangle. Trace the patterns from page 52. Cut and arrange the other wool pieces as directed below.
3. From gold wool, cut one lace 1 and one lace 2. Use lace 3 as a template if lace 2 needs to be longer.
4. From green wool, cut one small and two large leaves, and eight ½" x 6" strips for stems.
5. From gold wool, cut one extra-large circle, five medium circles, and two small circles.
6. From the red wool, cut one extra-large, two large, and two tiny circles.
7. From the black wool, cut one medium and four tiny circles.
8. From the blue wool, cut one medium and one small circle.

ASSEMBLY AND APPLIQUÉ

1. Referring to the photograph and Diagram A for placement, position the crazy quilt pieces on the black background beginning with the cream rectangle; pin in place.

2. Building around the cream rectangle and moving outward, cut and pin down wool pieces in color, sizes, and shapes of your choice, with edges butting together or overlapping slightly, and leaving a black border all around the crazy-quilt center.

3. Using black wool thread, stitch the outside edges of the crazy quilt section to the black wool background with large primitive X's.

X XXX XXXX

4. Using black wool thread, stitch all the edges of the crazy quilt pieces to the black background with a funky zig-zag stitch.

∿∿∿∿∿∿

5. Using black thread, whipstitch two lace pieces where desired.

6. Trace the large heart and both star patterns onto some of the wool pieces on the crazy-quilt section. Carefully cut each shape out of the fabric, as if cutting a stencil, making sure not to cut through the black background. Using black thread, whipstitch the edges of the cutout areas to the black background.

DIAGRAM A

7. Refer to the photograph and Diagram A to arrange some of the green stems on the cream-color rectangle. Using black wool thread, whipstitch the stems in place.

8. Whipstitch the flower centers onto the flowers. Then whipstitch the flowers at the end of the stems.

9. Arrange the remaining stems, leaves, and flowers on other wool sections; whipstitch in place.

10. Lay the backing piece on the appliquéd top with right sides together. Sew along the outside edges with a ½" seam allowance, leaving a 5" opening on one side; turn right side out and press. Sew the opening closed.

Vest

MATERIALS

- One gray wool button-front vest with two front pockets
- Scraps of green boiled wool and gold, cream, red, and blue wool for appliqué
- Cream and black embroidery floss

CUTTING

1. Trace patterns from page 52. From the green boiled wool, cut a ½" x 2" strip for stems, and four small leaves.

2. For each flower, cut one large circle from a different color of boiled wool.

3. From gold wool, cut two pieces of lace using whichever pattern fits the width of the pocket; adjust if necessary.

APPLIQUÉ AND FINISHING

1. Using six strands of cream embroidery floss, blanket-stitch around each pocket.

2. Referring to the photograph for placement, position stems and leaves below each buttonhole. Using black

embroidery floss, blanket-stitch stems and leaves in place.

3. Blanket-stitch around the edge of each circle. Cut a slash in the center of each circle the size of the buttonhole; whipstitch circles to the vest.

4. Using six strands of black embroidery floss, blanket-stitch a gold lace piece to the top of each pocket and blanket-stitch along vest edges.

1. Trace patterns from page 52. From gold wool, cut a piece of lace to fit around the top edge of one shoe, and also cut a large star.
2. From red wool, cut a large circle, a large star, and a small heart.
3. From the green boiled wool, cut two large leaves.

APPLIQUÉ AND DECORATION

1. Using six strands of cream embroidery floss, blanket-stitch lace to the top edge of one shoe.
2. Using six strands of cream embroidery floss, blanket-stitch around all the appliqué pieces. Randomly hot-glue pieces to the shoes including a heart at the back of one shoe.
3. Using six strands of cream embroidery floss, blanket-stitch along the top edge and the opening of the other shoe.

Fancy Footwork

MATERIALS

- Black canvas high-top tennis shoes
- Scraps of gold, red, and blue wool and green boiled wool for appliqué
- Cream embroidery floss

HANDSOME GLOVES

Purchased gloves become handsome accessories when you add wool flowers, stems, hearts, and stars from the appliqué patterns featured on the shoes and the wallhanging. Blanket-stitch the appliqués onto the gloves with black floss.

Rug-Hooked Flower

Finished size 9" x 11"

MATERIALS

- 12" x 14" piece of angus cloth (rug-hooking burlap)
- 9" x 11" piece of black wool
- 18" long strips of skirt-weight wool in the following widths and colors: 6" green, 4" gold, 2" red, 2" black, 10" cream
- 12" length of wire

CUTTING

1. Cut the assorted pieces of skirt-weight wool into ¼" wide strips.

HOOKING AND FINISHING

1. Transfer the hooked rug design, page 53, to the center of the angus cloth.
2. Referring to the instructions on page 53, hook the flowers first, then the stems.
3. Hook the background, forming an 8" x 10" rectangle.
4. Trim the excess angus cloth, but allow a 1" margin for the hem.
5. Fold under the hem; steam-press to the back of the hooked piece.
6. Glue the black wool rectangle to the back of the hooked piece. Place a heavy book on top of the piece until the glue dries. Trim edges of black wool with pinking shears.
7. Twist the wire and attach to the two top corners for hanging.

BOWLER IN BLOOM

For a hat brimming with blooms, blanket-stitch around the appliqués, add buttons where desired, and then hot glue the appliqués to the hat.

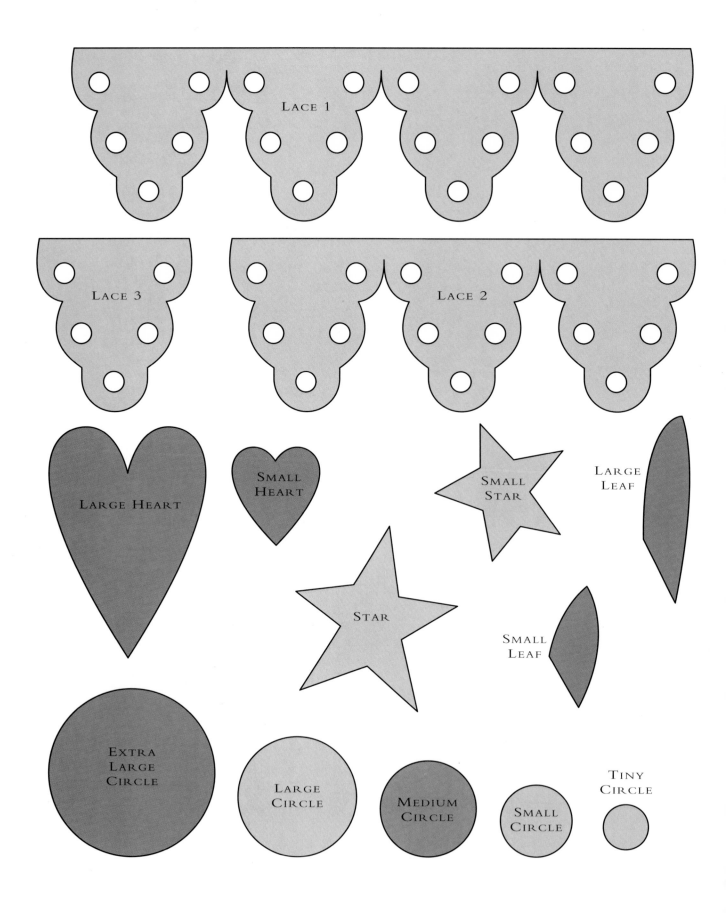

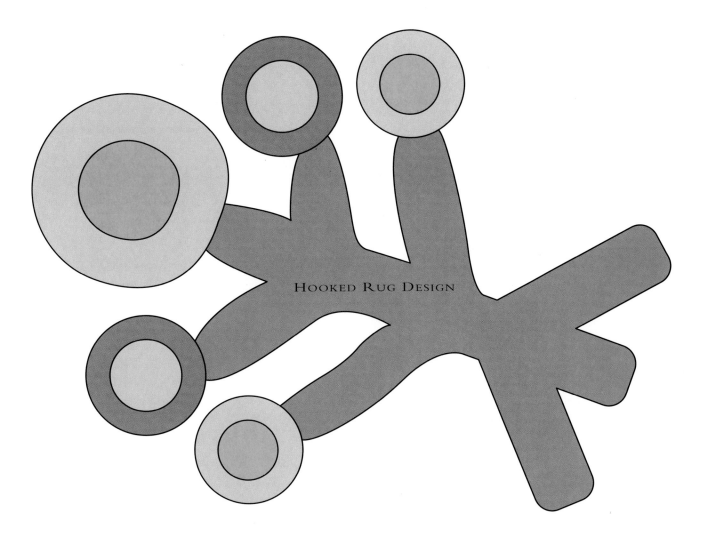

HOOKED RUG DESIGN

HOOKING A RUG

1. Transfer the design to the center of the angus cloth (burlap mesh). Stretch the cloth in a hoop. Hold the wool strip underneath the burlap between the thumb and forefinger of your left hand. Hold the rug hook above the burlap in your right hand. Push the hook through the mesh of the burlap. With the shaft of the hook touching your left finger, slide behind the strip and, with help of the thumb, pick up the strip. Pull the hook up, pulling the end of the strip through the mesh ½".

2. Push the hook into the next hole in the mesh; catch the strip and pull up a loop to a height of ¼", or until the height equals the width of the strip. Depending on the burlap mesh and the width of your strips, you may not need to hook in every hole—wider strips must be spaced farther apart.

3. Pull the end of the strip or the last of a color to the top and trim to ½". Start a second strip or another color in the same hole. Trim the ends even with the loops when finished.

4. To keep the project from getting lumpy, don't float your strip under an already hooked section. Instead, cut the strip and start again on the other side. When starting a new row, move over as many holes as necessary to accommodate the width of the strip.

Patrice Longmire

FROM MY HEART TO YOURS

For Patrice Longmire, her signature quote, "From my heart to yours," is a thread that pulls at the heartstrings of the many devoted stitchers who purchase their patterns from Patrice & Company's extensive offering of designs.

Many seek out her one-of-a-kind dolls as well as her quick-sew collection of quilts in a myriad of shapes and sizes—from wall to wallet size.

Others are inspired by the primitive designs and captivating phrases that fill the pages of Patrice's nationally-distributed books, which number 13 and counting!

The wide range of projects you'll find on the following pages are derived from Patrice's quick-sew wallhanging, shown opposite. Special features of the whimsical wallhanging are an embroidered phrase from the Bible: "All creatures great and small," and a quote adapted from the title of the song: "Let there be peace on earth and let it begin with me," which inspired the accompanying host of heavenly motifs—a folk-style angel, moon, and stars.

Whether you choose to begin with the wallhanging or something smaller—like the sweet face of an angel painted on a garden stake or embroidered on a petite pillow—the results will be so rewarding, you'll truly be able to "count your blessings!"

MATERIALS

- ⅓ yard each of black plaid fabric and gold stripe flannel for background
- ½ yard of brown stripe flannel for background
- ¼ yard each of brown print, green plaid, and red-and-olive green plaid flannel for background
- ½ yard of green flannel for stems and borders
- 1⅜ yards of fabric for backing
- ⅜ yard of red plaid flannel for binding
- Assorted scraps of flannel in black, off-white, gold print, red check, red plaid, brown check and pink stripe for appliqué
- Rose and peach wool felt
- Off-white and black pearl cotton thread
- 1⅜ yards of batting
- Powder blush for angel's cheeks

Quick-Sew Wallhanging

Finished size 38" x 51"

CUTTING

1. From black plaid, cut a 10" x 26½" rectangle (A).
2. From brown stripe fabric, cut a 4½" x 26½" (B) and a 7" x 35" (G) strip.
3. From brown print fabric, cut a 6½" x 26½" strip (C).
4. From green plaid fabric, cut a 9" x 20" strip (D).
5. From gold stripe fabric, cut a 16" x 35" rectangle (E).
6. From red-and-olive green plaid fabric, cut a 7" x 35" strip (F).
7. From green flannel, cut five 2½" strips across the width for borders.
8. From red plaid fabric, cut five 2½" strips across the width for binding.
9. Referring to the General Instructions on page 6, trace, apply fusible web to, and cut out the following appliqué pieces on pages 61–65: Six stems, five stems in reverse, four large hearts, three flowerpots, three large stars, two cats, and one each bluebird, medium star, moon, large angel wing, hair, face, and dress.
10. From the rose felt, cut seven flowers and four centers. From the peach felt, cut four flowers and seven centers.

PIECING AND APPLIQUÉ

1. Referring to Diagram A, right, and instructions below, assemble quilt top.

2. Sew together pieces A, B, and C; add D to the right side; add E, F, and G.

3. Cut one of the border strips in half; sew each half to an end of two of the other strips. Sew long strips to the long side edges of the quilt top; trim ends even. Sew remaining border strips to the top and bottom edges of the quilt top; trim.

4. Referring to the photograph on page 55 and the directions below, position and fuse appliqué pieces to quilt top. If desired, machine-appliqué edges.

5. Fuse stems, leaving space for the flowers and pots. Fuse the angel wings and hair, and then the face and dress. Fuse the cats, stars, hearts, moon, and bird.

6. Using cream pearl cotton thread, attach flowers and flower centers to the quilt top with French knots, blanket stitches, and running stitches.

7. Using a silver quilter's pencil, mark the following phrases: "All Creatures Great And Small" and "Let there be Peace on Earth and let it begin with Me!"

8. Using black pearl cotton thread, backstitch the first phrase, bird's legs, and cats' whiskers. Make French knots for the cats' and bird's eyes. Using cream pearl cotton thread, backstitch the second phrase.

9. Apply blush to angel's face for cheeks.

FINISHING

1. Referring to the General Instructions on page 7, layer the wallhanging.

2. Quilt about ¼" away from all seam lines except in the border. Quilt about ¼" away from the appliqué pieces.

3. Sew binding strips into one long strip; bind the wallhanging following the General Instructions on page 7.

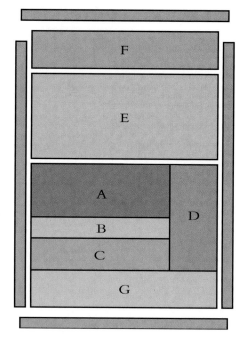

DIAGRAM A

Angel Pillow
7" x 10" pillow

MATERIALS

- ½ yard of muslin for pillow top and backing
- Green, red, and gold scraps of wool for borders and pillow back
- Olive green, red, and brown embroidery floss
- Fade-away marker
- Powder blush for angel's cheeks
- 8" x 11" piece of thin quilt batting
- Polyester stuffing

CUTTING

1. Cut two 2" x 8" border strips from olive green fabric, and one 2" x 8" strip each from red and gold fabric.

2. Cut one 8" x 11" rectangle of wool for back, one of batting, and two of muslin.

1. Using the fabric marker, draw a 5" x 8" rectangle in the center of one piece of the muslin.

2. Using a fade-away marker, trace the angel pattern on page 69 to the center of the rectangle.

3. Using two strands of floss, backstitch the lettering, heart, and lips with red; the hair, face outline, eyes, nose, and dimple with brown; and the leaves with green.

4. Apply blush to angel's face for cheeks.

5. Cut out the 5" x 8" rectangle. Sew green borders to top and bottom edges of rectangle; press seam allowances toward strips. Sew red and gold border strips to side edges of muslin rectangle; press seam allowances.

6. Layer backing, batting, and pillow top. Quilt ¼" inside the muslin rectangle. Quilt diagonal lines in the border.

7. Place quilted pillow top and wool pillow back with right sides together.

8. Sew together leaving an opening on the side. Trim corners; turn right side out. Stuff pillow, filling corners first. Slip-stitch opening closed.

GINGERBREAD PALS GARLAND

Gather your favorite flannels. Trace the pattern from page 68 onto doubled layers of fabric with right sides out. Stitch around pattern leaving an opening along one side. Cut out shape ⅛" beyond the stitching. Stuff; backstitch openings closed. Cut small hearts from thin metal, wood, or cardboard; paint and antique. Tie raffia or jute bows around the necks and attach the hearts. Thread the fabric pals together with a length of jute.

14" doll

MATERIALS

- ⅓ yard of muslin for body
- ⅜ yard of brown plaid fabric for dress
- ⅜ yard of red plaid fabric for pantaloons
- Scrap of red wool for heart
- Black and red embroidery floss for face and hand-sewing
- Polyester stuffing
- Four small white buttons
- 10 to 12 whole cloves for hair
- Black permanent fabric marker
- Fade-away fabric marker
- Powder blush for cheeks
- Gold acrylic paint and antiquing medium
- 6" x 8" piece of aluminum flashing or cardboard for wings

BODY

1. Trace two each of arms and legs and one body pattern piece from page 67 on double layer of muslin.
2. Sew on traced lines, leaving open where indicated on pattern. Cut out pieces ⅛" beyond stitching lines.
3. Turn pieces right side out. Stuff arms and legs to within 2" from top. Stuff head and shoulder area of the body.
4. Referring to Diagram B, draw the angel face with a fade-away marker. For all hand sewing, begin and end stitches through an unstuffed portion of the body. Using two strands of black floss, stitch the nose, making one long loose stitch down and one short stitch at the bottom creating an "L" shape. Make

French knots for the eyes and add a single stitch over each eye for eyebrows. Satin-stitch the mouth with red floss; outline mouth with back-stitches to define the lips.

5. Apply powder blush to the face for cheeks. Using a permanent marker, draw small random freckle dots on the cheeks.
6. Stuff the remaining portion of the body.
7. Sew body, arm, and leg openings closed.
8. Using gold paint, paint shoes onto each foot; let dry. Hot-glue a small button to top of each shoe.
9. Apply hot glue to top of each arm; press onto body, and hold until glue has cooled. Apply glue to top of each leg; press onto body. Arms and legs are floppy to allow for easy positioning.
10. For hair, remove the ball at the end of each clove. Hot-glue the clove stems evenly spaced along the seam line of the head.

DIAGRAM B

PANTALOONS

1. Trace, and cut two pantaloons on fold.

2. Sew a ½" hem in bottom of each leg.

3. With right sides together, sew crotch seams (Diagram C).

4. With right sides together, match front and back crotch seams; stitch inseam. Clip curves (Diagram D).

5. Turn right side out and press under ½" waist hem; stitch. Thread embroidery floss through waist hem.

6. Place pantaloons on angel. Draw up floss snug around waist, and tie.

DRESS

1. Trace and cut two bodice pieces on fold; open flat and press.

2. Place bodice pieces with right sides together; sew upper sleeve seams from wrist edge to neck notch. Clip where indicated on pattern and open out.

3. Sew a ½" hem in bottom of each sleeve.

4. Place bodice pieces with right sides together; sew underarm and side seams. Clip as indicated on pattern; turn right side out. Press under ¼" at neck edges.

5. For the dress skirt, cut a 7½" x 15" rectangle of dress fabric. Sew a ½" hem in one long edge.

6. With the right sides together, sew the 7½" back seam of skirt.

7. Sew a gathering stitch along top raw edge of skirt. With right sides together, pin skirt to bodice and adjust gathers evenly spaced around bodice.

8. Sew skirt to bodice. Turn the dress right side out.

9. Using floss, hand-sew a gathering stitch around neck edge.

10. Place dress on angel. Snug up gathers around neck edge, knot and clip the ends of floss.

11. Hot-glue two buttons to the front of the dress.

DIAGRAM C

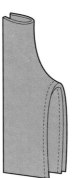

DIAGRAM D

HEART NECKLACE

1. Trace necklace heart pattern on doubled red wool.

2. Sew around heart on traced line. Cut out heart ⅛" beyond the stitching line.

3. Cut a small slash in one side of the heart. Turn heart right side out and stuff lightly. Slip-stitch opening closed.

4. Thread a strand of embroidery floss, jute, or pearl cotton thread through the back side of the heart (the side with the slash). Tie the necklace around angel's neck at desired length. Tie a knot and clip the ends of the floss.

WINGS

1. Trace doll wing pattern onto metal or cardboard and cut out with scissors.

2. Apply sealer to metal wings; let dry. Paint metal with acrylic paint; let dry. To give wings an aged look, apply an antique finish and let dry.

3. To poke holes around the outer edge of the wings, place wings on a block of wood. Place a nail where you want to make a hole. Tap head of nail hard enough to puncture the metal.

4. Place the wings on the back of the angel. Using sturdy thread, hand-sew wings to angel by sewing through the holes at the center top of the wings and through the back of the head. Tie thread in a knot and clip the ends.

Garden Gift Bag

8½" x 11" bag

MATERIALS

- ⅔ yard of red check flannel for bag
- ¼ yard of muslin for background
- Small scrap of rose wool for heart
- Nine assorted buttons
- Ecru, light cinnamon, green, and gold embroidery floss
- Fade-away fabric marker

CUTTING

1. Cut two 9" x 15" rectangles from the red check flannel.
2. Cut two 5½" x 8½" rectangles from the muslin.
3. Trace heart on page 69 and cut out from rose wool.

GARDEN SIGN

Cut a 5½" x 8" piece of ½" wood. Sand, seal, and then paint off-white. Place graphite or carbon paper on wood. Center and transfer design from page 69. With a fine brush, add the details on the design using red, brown, and green paints. When paint is dry, antique and then seal. Nail the painted wood piece to a painted and sealed garden stake.

DECORATING AND ASSEMBLY

1. Use a fade-away marker to trace design on page 69 onto one muslin rectangle.
2. With right sides together, sew muslin pieces together, leaving an opening for turning. Turn right side out; press. Stitch opening closed.
3. Using embroidery floss, sew heart onto muslin; backstitch lettering and flowers.
4. Using running stitches, sew muslin block centered near bottom on one flannel rectangle. Decorate with buttons.
5. Place flannel rectangles with right sides together; sew one 15" side edge. Sew a 3" hem in the top edge. Sew together opposite edge and bottom of bag. Turn and press.

Snowman Gift Bag

1. Referring to materials and instructions for Garden Gift Bag, make a basic bag.
2. Refer to the General Instructions on page 6 to trace, apply fusible web to, and cut out one snowman and wings; birdhouse, hole, roof, and post; and four small stars on page 63. Fuse.
3. Use black floss for decorative stitches and attaching buttons. Make French knots for eyes and mouth and satin-stitch nose. Apply blush to face for cheeks.

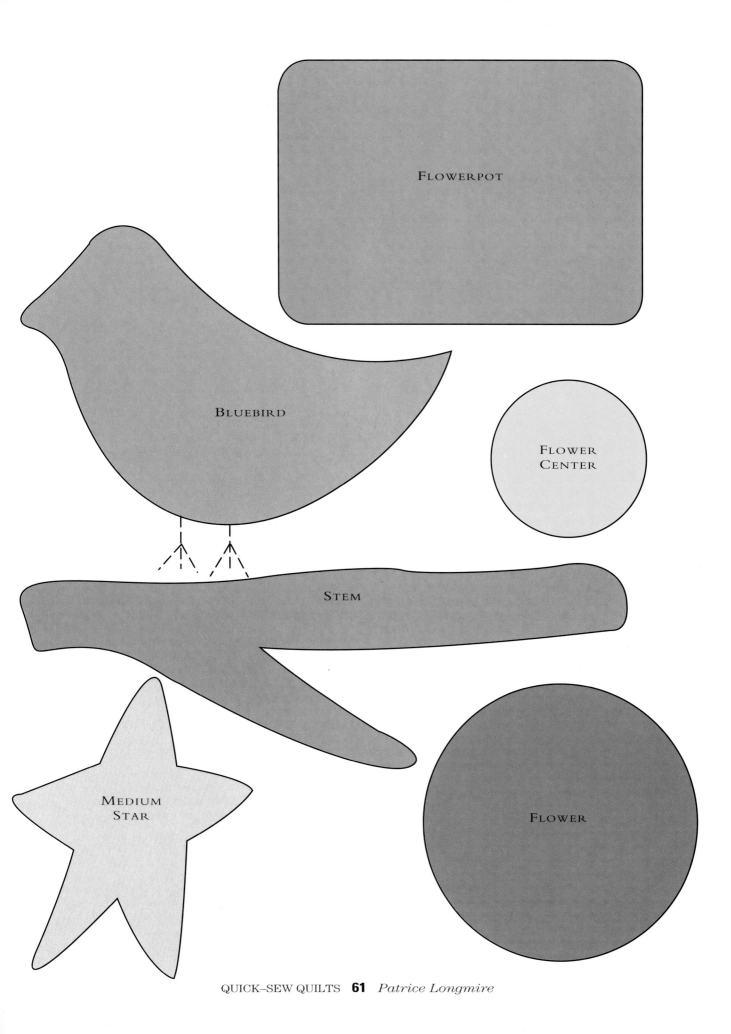

FLOWERPOT

BLUEBIRD

FLOWER
CENTER

STEM

MEDIUM
STAR

FLOWER

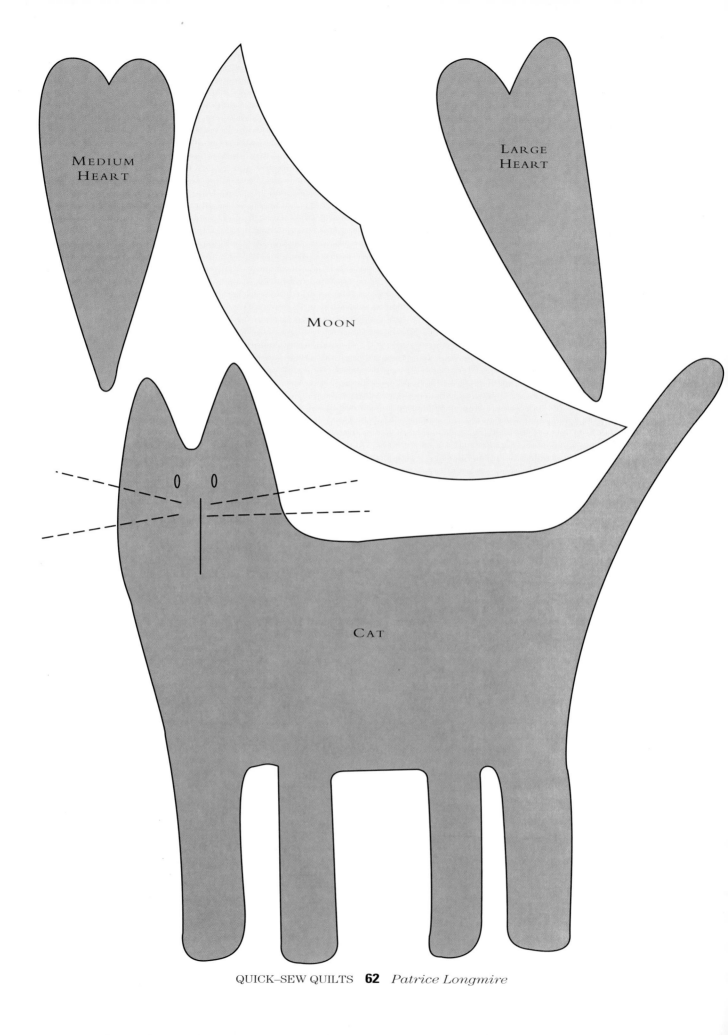

MEDIUM HEART

LARGE HEART

MOON

CAT

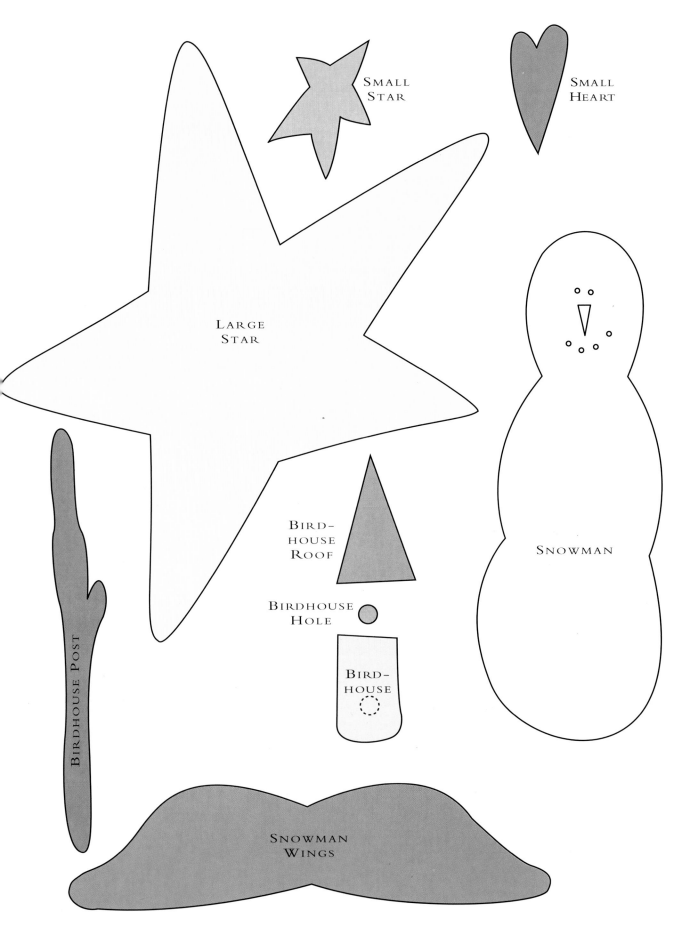

SMALL STAR

SMALL HEART

LARGE STAR

SNOWMAN

BIRD– HOUSE ROOF

BIRDHOUSE HOLE

BIRD– HOUSE

BIRDHOUSE POST

SNOWMAN WINGS

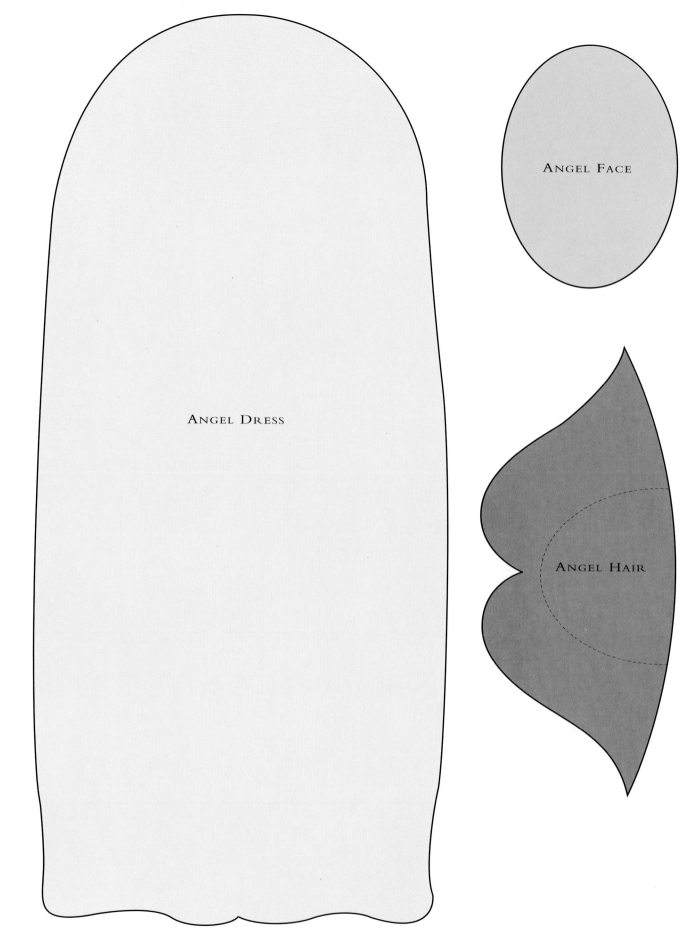

ANGEL FACE

ANGEL DRESS

ANGEL HAIR

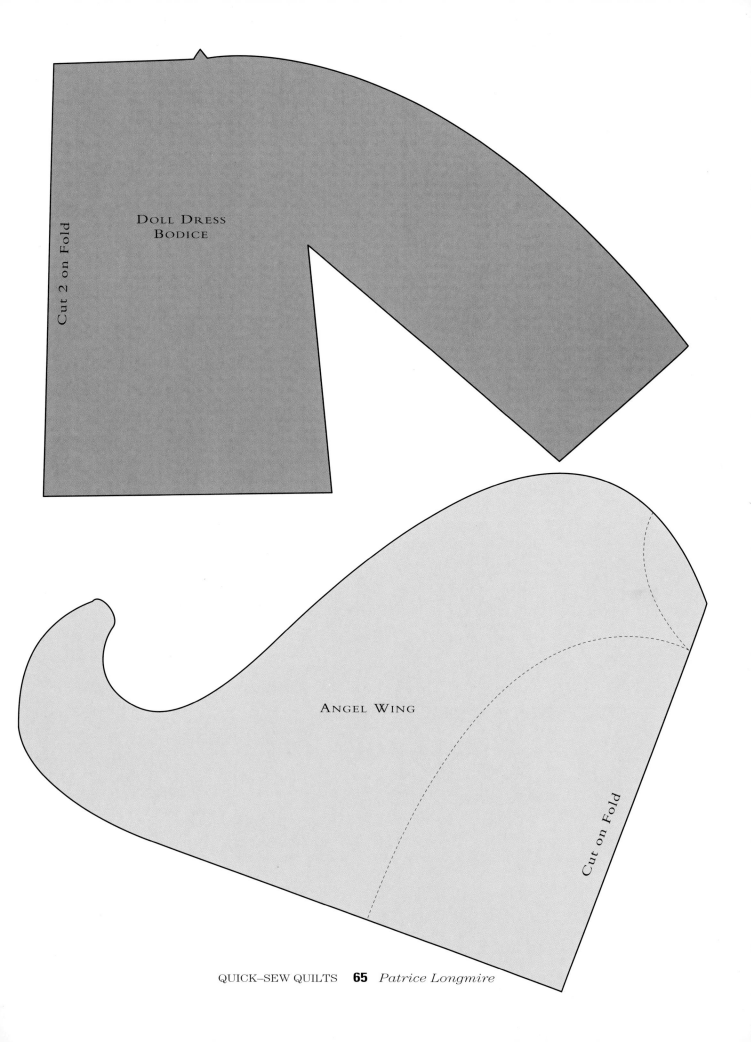

Doll Dress
Bodice

Cut 2 on Fold

Angel Wing

Cut on Fold

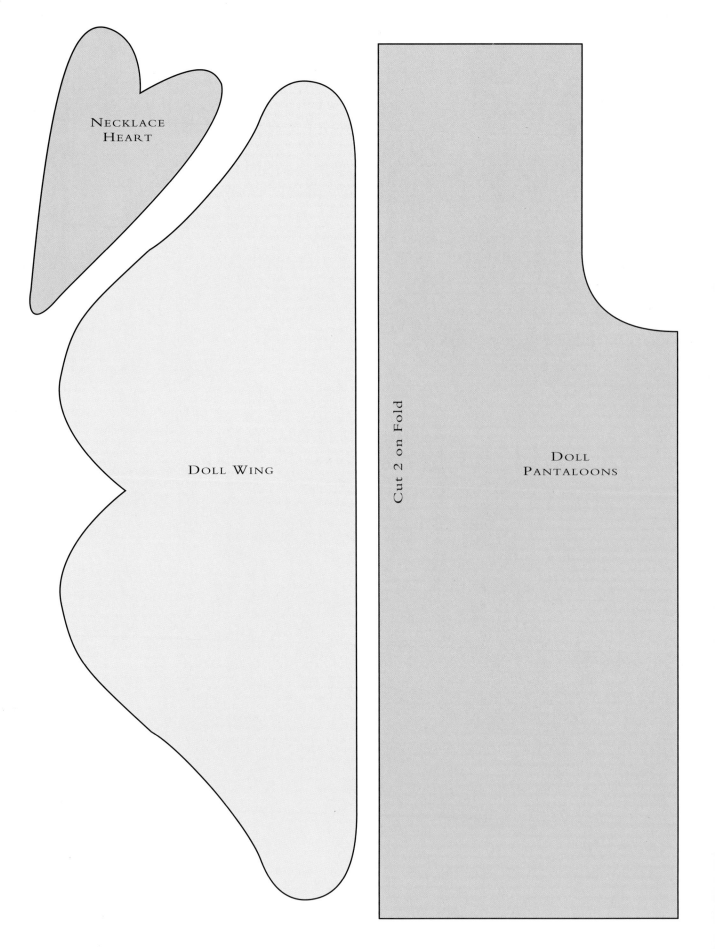

NECKLACE
HEART

DOLL WING

Cut 2 on Fold

DOLL
PANTALOONS

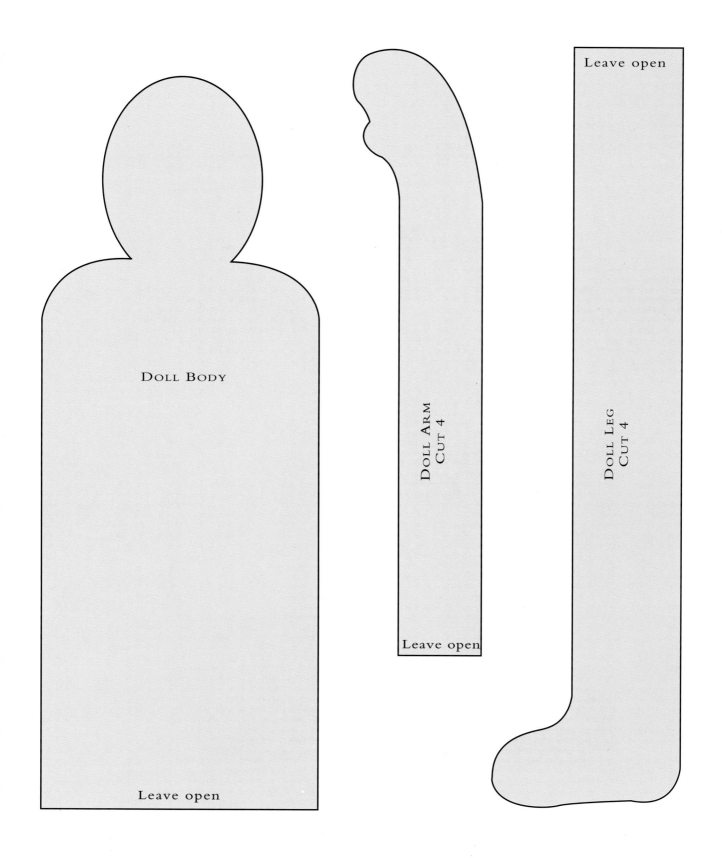

Doll Body

Leave open

Doll Arm
Cut 4

Leave open

Leave open

Doll Leg
Cut 4

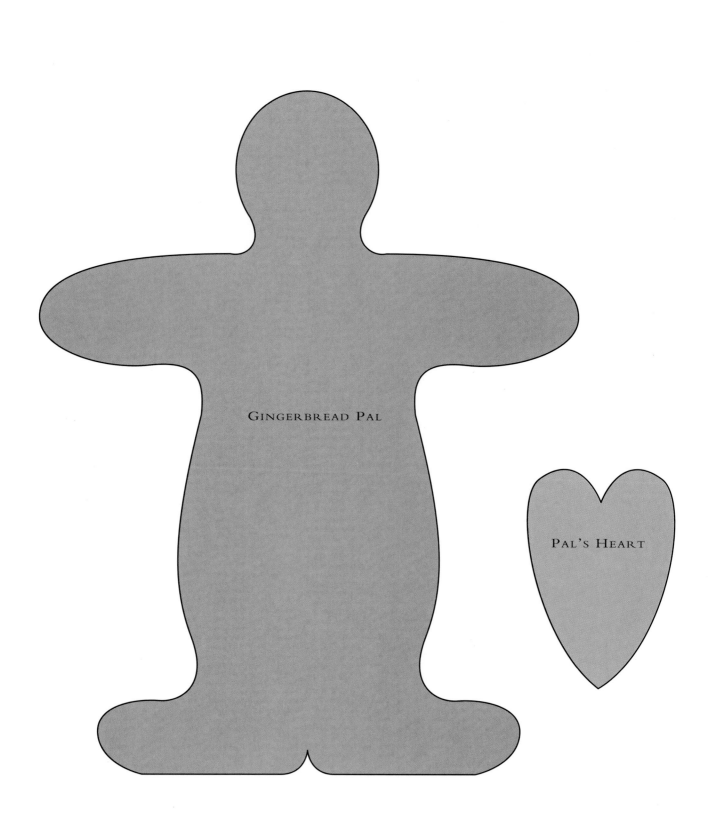

GINGERBREAD PAL

PAL'S HEART

Plant

Kindness

Gather

Love

GIFT BAG
HEART

blessings

McKenna Ryan

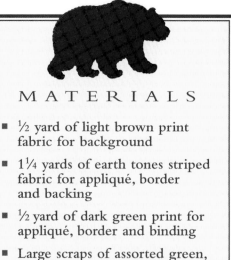

The day after her wedding, McKenna Ryan traded the snowy shores of Lake Michigan for the mountain avalanches of Northern Montana, sight unseen! With her husband, Vince, McKenna experienced firsthand the harshest of living conditions combined with almost total isolation. McKenna began making quilts for her family and friends featuring grizzlies, moose, and other creatures. During a trip to New Mexico, McKenna stopped at a small shop to get inspiration for her handmade quilts.

After only a few minutes, she ran back out to the car and excitedly said to Vince, "Honey, I need $6. I'm going to buy a pattern—I know what I'm going to do!"

With Vince as her strongest supporter, McKenna spent an entire year developing her first line of original "Quilt Designs by Pine Needles." To compete with patterns already on the market, she created distinct packaging—brown paper bags with raffia ties. Her first show was followed by the Houston Quilt Market—a show so successful she's been back every year since.

Even on the most difficult days, McKenna clings to her motto, "Out of every diversity comes a gift." As you are inspired by McKenna's Northwoods designs shown here and on the following pages, let them be her gift to you!

MATERIALS

- ½ yard of light brown print fabric for background
- 1¼ yards of earth tones striped fabric for appliqué, border and backing
- ½ yard of dark green print for appliqué, border and binding
- Large scraps of assorted green, gold, dark brown and striped prints; and blue, green, gold and multi-colored plaids
- Fusible web
- 26" x 36" piece of batting
- Invisible thread
- Gold embroidery floss

Quick-Sew Wallhanging

Finished size 25" x 32"

CUTTING

1. From the light brown print background fabric cut a 17½" x 24½" rectangle.
2. From the earth tones striped fabric cut two 3" x 26" and two 3" x 24" border strips across the stripe pattern. Then, cut a 27" x 34" backing rectangle.
3. From dark green print fabric, cut two 1¼" x 19" and two 1¼" x 24½" border strips. Cut four 2½" binding strips across width of fabric. Cut a 3½" x 27" strip for tabs.
4. Refer to the General Instructions on page 6 to trace, apply fusible web to, and cut out the following appliqué pieces on pages 76–80: One each pond (connect both patterns), moon, moose, antlers, canoe, diamond, base log, large log, window, candle, flame, chimney, smoke, roof, eagle, eagle tail, and eagle head; two each pine tree, arrowhead, paddle, shutter, shutter tree, and muntin; and five each medium and small logs.

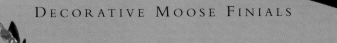

DECORATIVE MOOSE FINIALS

Make your completed wallhanging a conversation piece by adding

a whimsical woodland finial to each end of a ⅝" dowel.

The moose shown here is one of a purchased pair (see Sources).

PIECING AND ASSEMBLY

1. Referring to Diagram A, assemble the top as follows: Sew 24½" green border strips to top and bottom edges of background rectangle. Press seam allowances toward strips. Sew 19" green strips to side edges; press seam allowances. Sew 26" striped strips to top and bottom edges; press seam allowances. Sew 24" striped strips to side edges; press seam allowances.

2. Referring to the photograph on page 71 and directions below, fuse appliqué pieces to print background, layering as indicated by dashed lines on patterns.

3. Position lower left corner of window 7½" from bottom edge and 10" from left edge of the background; fuse. Fuse muntins. Fuse large log, overlapping bottom of window; fuse remaining logs. Fuse roof, slipping bottom edge of chimney underneath roof edge. Fuse smoke. Fuse trees to shutters.

4. Position pond, canoe pieces, and paddles; fuse. Add moose, slipping antlers under head. Position and fuse the moon, trees, and eagle pieces.

5. Fold the hanging-tab strip in half lengthwise with wrong sides together; sew with a ¼" seam allowance. Open strip and press flat with seam in center; (Diagram B). Cut strip into three 9" sections for tabs.

FINISHING

1. Referring to the General Instructions on page 7, layer the wallhanging.

2. Using invisible thread, stitch just outside all appliqué pieces. Stitch inside both edges of the green border.

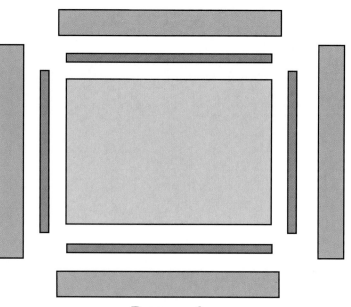

DIAGRAM A

DIAGRAM B

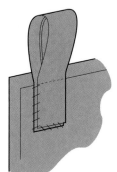

DIAGRAM C

3. Trim edges of layers even. Sew the four 2½" binding strips into one long strip. Fold strip wrong sides together; press. Pin binding strip against quilt front with raw edges matching. Referring to the General Instructions on page 7 for straight corners, sew binding in place using a ¼" seam allowance. Turn binding to back; whipstitch in place.

4. Trace three small fish to fusible web and fuse to wrong side of plaid fabric; cut out. Fuse to wrong side of another piece of same fabric; cut out. Attach fish near the roof line with 6 strands of gold floss. Embroider eagle's beak with gold floss.

5. Fold each tab section in half crosswise with seam centered on the inside. Position tabs at each end and in center of top edge of wallhanging, overlapping the back about 1½". Sew crosswise along the binding seam. Whipstitch the sides and lower portion in place (Diagram C).

MATERIALS

- 12" square of dark green wool for background
- 12" scrap of light green wool for tree
- Gold, red-brown, and blue wool scraps for appliqué
- 1 yard of heavyweight striped fabric for pillow front and back
- Six 1" red buttons
- Green thread
- Gold embroidery floss
- 18" square pillow form

CUTTING

1. Refer to the General Instructions on page 6 to trace, apply fusible web to, and cut the following appliqué pieces on pages 76, 77, 81 and 83: Tall tree, bear, star and moon.

2. With the stripes going the long way, cut a 20" x 37" rectangle from the pillow fabric.

APPLIQUÉ

1. Referring to the photograph, fuse appliqué pieces to green wool; first the moon, then the tall tree, bear, and star.

2. Using black pearl cotton thread, blanket-stitch along exposed edges of the appliqué pieces.

3. Using gold embroidery floss, sew running stitches about ¼" from the edges of the star.

DIAGRAM D

ASSEMBLY AND FINISHING

1. Fold the rectangle in half with wrong sides together so cover is 20" x 18½".

2. Center and pin the appliquéd square to one layer of the folded pillow cover, 3" below the folded edge. Be sure to allow for a ½" seam allowance along the unsewn bottom pillow edge.

3. Using 6 strands of gold floss and running stitches, sew the square in place, sewing about ¼" in from the edges.

4. Refold the rectangle with right sides together and sew the raw edges together with ½" seam allowances, leaving a large opening in the bottom edge for turning and for inserting the pillow form. Turn the pillow cover right side out.

5. Sew three buttons about ¾" from each side edge and spaced about 6" apart from the center button. Insert the pillow form. Whip-stitch the opening closed.

Grapevine Wreath

18" wreath

MATERIALS

- Assorted large fabric scraps in green, light brown and red print; and light green and dark green plaids and stripes for stuffed ornaments
- Small scrap of blue plaid fabric for appliqué
- ¼ yard of red print for bow
- Fusible web
- Freezer paper
- Polyester stuffing
- 18" grapevine wreath
- Brown embroidery floss

CUTTING

1. Trace the following appliqué patterns from page 81 onto the dull side of freezer paper: three stars, two fish and two pine trees. Cut out templates.

2. Refer to the General Instructions on page 7 to trace, fuse and cut out the bluebird and small moose on page 81.

3. With pinking shears, cut a 4" x 44" strip of red print for the bow. Cut another strip about ¾" x 8".

ASSEMBLY AND FINISHING

1. For the stuffed stars, fish and trees, fold the chosen fabric, wrong sides together and iron the freezer paper template onto one right side of the fabric. Sew around the edges of the template, leaving a 2" opening on one side (Diagram E). Remove freezer paper. Stuff lightly with polyester stuffing. Finish sewing seams. With pinking shears, cut around the ornaments ¼" from the seam lines.

DIAGRAM E

2. For the moose ornament, fold the background fabric in half, position and fuse the moose with the bluebird perched on one antler. Sew around the moose and the bluebird about ¼" away from the appliqué, leaving a 2" opening. Stuff lightly with polyester stuffing. Finish sewing the seam. With pinking shears, cut around the ornament about ¼" beyond the stitching line.

3. Tie the smaller red strip print into a bow; angle-cut the ends with pinking shears. Tack bow at moose's neck.

4. Using a hot glue gun, glue stars, fish, and trees to sides and top of wreath.

5. Tie larger red print strip into a bow around the bottom of the wreath; angle-cut the ends with pinking shears.

6. Using brown embroidery floss, hang the moose ornament from the top of the wreath.

Brown Paper Gift Bag

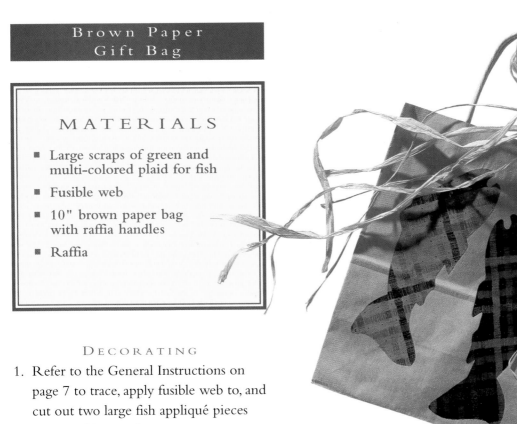

MATERIALS

- Large scraps of green and multi-colored plaid for fish
- Fusible web
- 10" brown paper bag with raffia handles
- Raffia

DECORATING

1. Refer to the General Instructions on page 7 to trace, apply fusible web to, and cut out two large fish appliqué pieces on page 81, reversing one.
2. Referring to the photograph, fuse the fish to the bag.
3. Fill bag and add a raffia bow to the handle.

NORTHWOODS STOCKINGS

Purchase a felt stocking or make one from your favorite pattern. Trace, fuse, and cut out felt animals and other shapes from the appliqué pieces in this chapter. Fuse them to the center of the stocking. Trace and cut out several Christmas trees and sew to stocking with buttons. Cut a 1½" felt strip about 10" long. Fold and cross over the ends. Attach loop to the upper back edge of the stocking with a button.

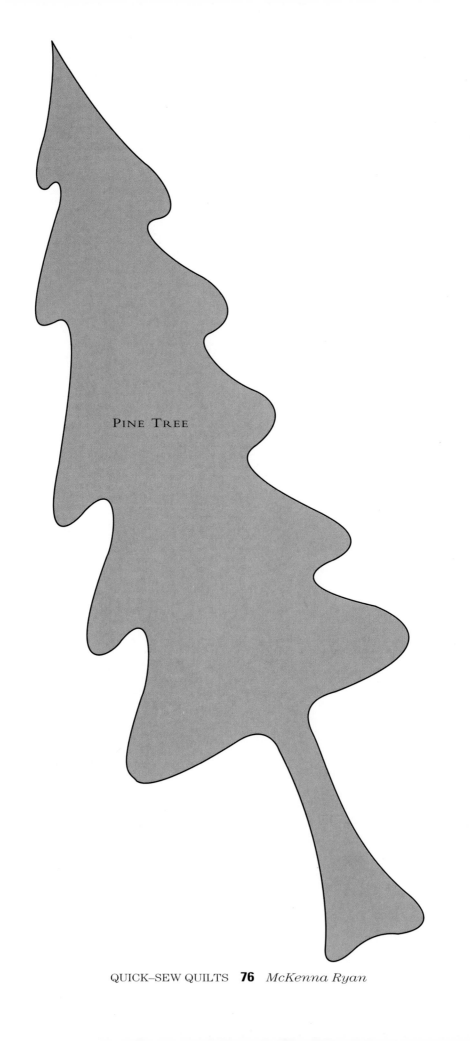

Pine Tree

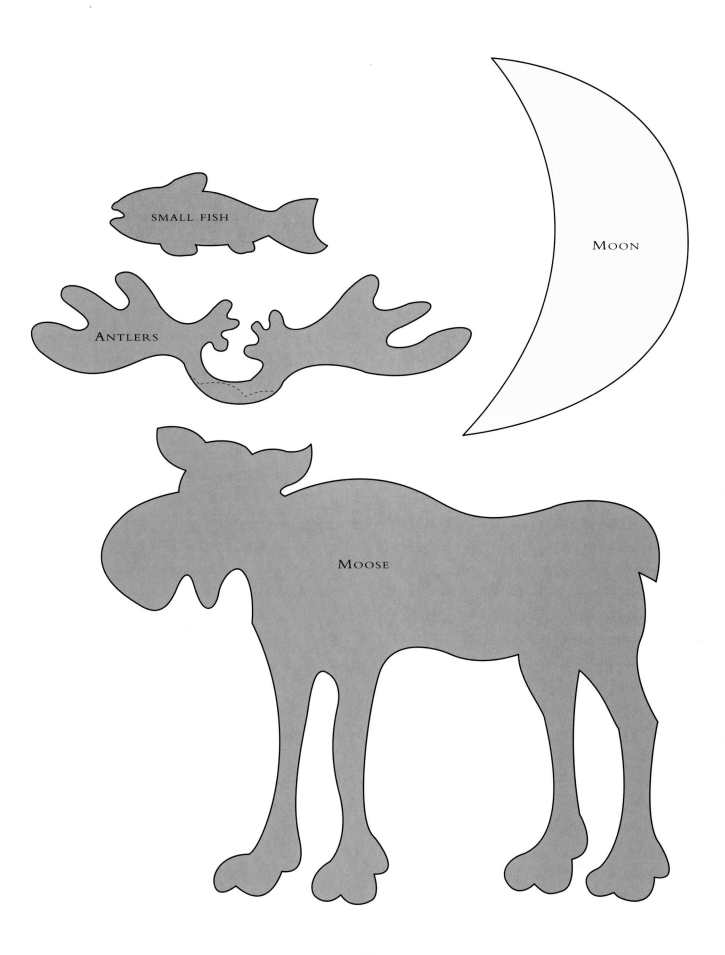

SMALL FISH

MOON

ANTLERS

MOOSE

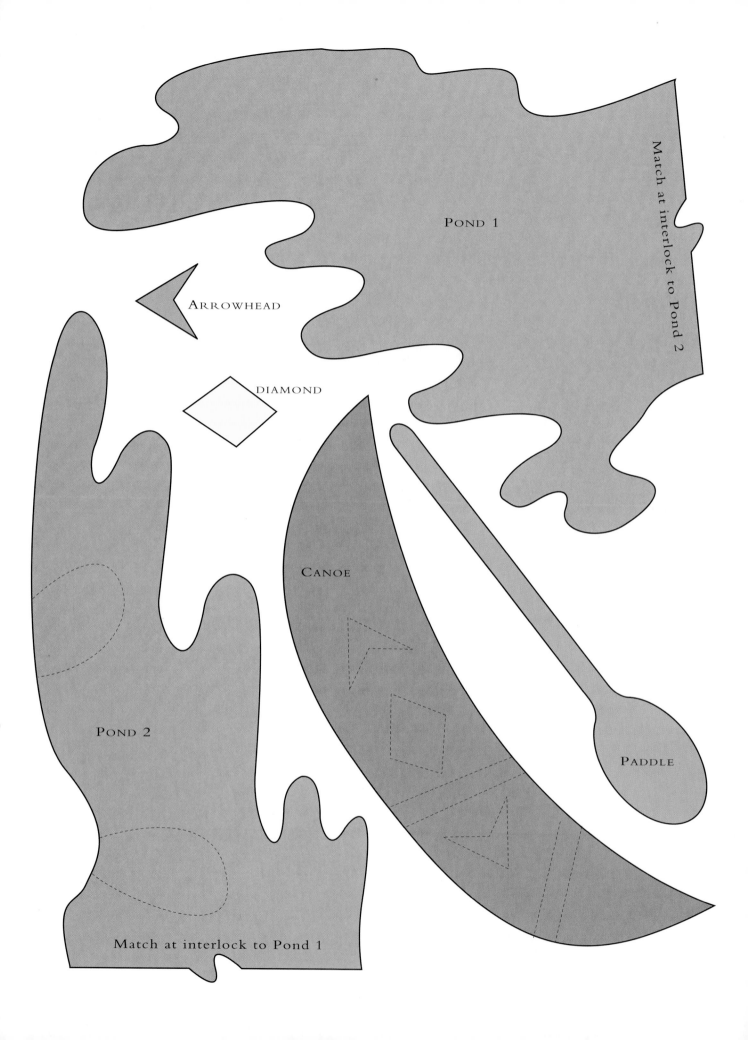

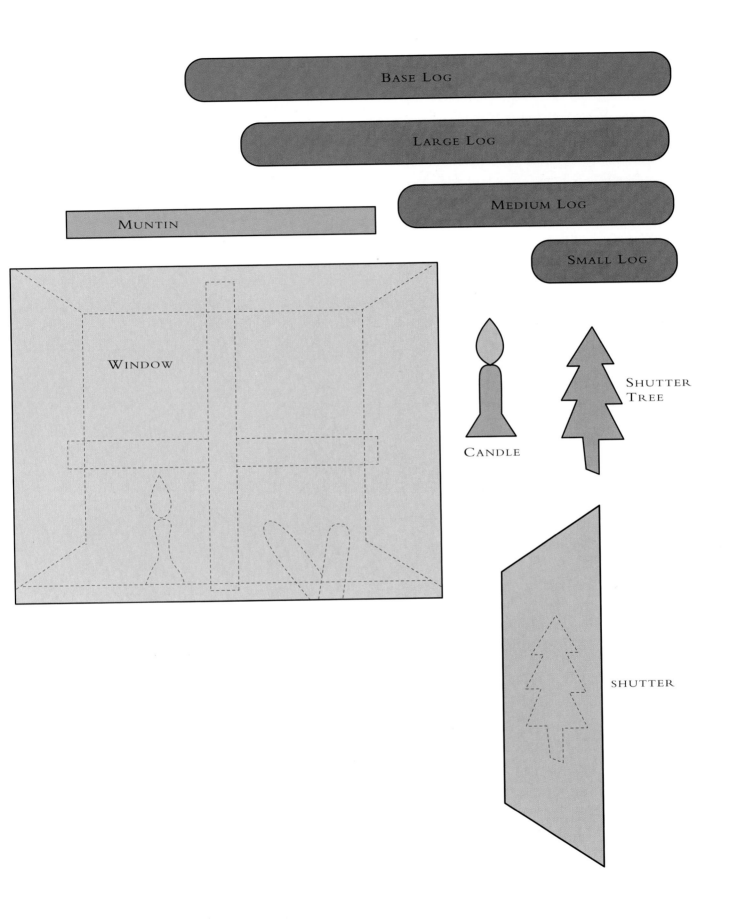

BASE LOG

LARGE LOG

MEDIUM LOG

MUNTIN

SMALL LOG

WINDOW

CANDLE

SHUTTER
TREE

SHUTTER

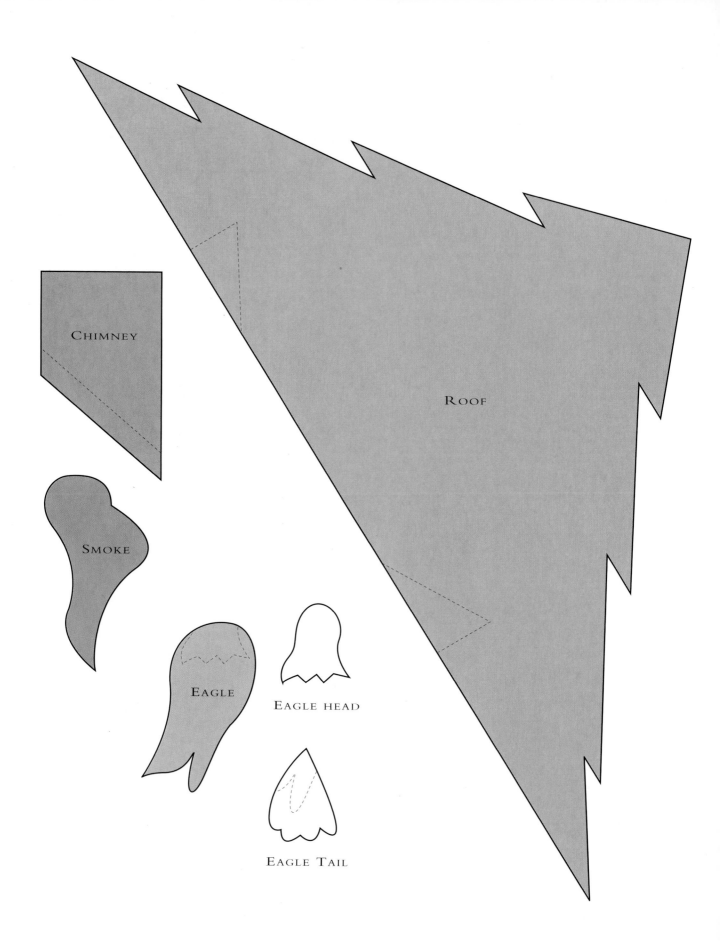

CHIMNEY

ROOF

SMOKE

EAGLE

EAGLE HEAD

EAGLE TAIL

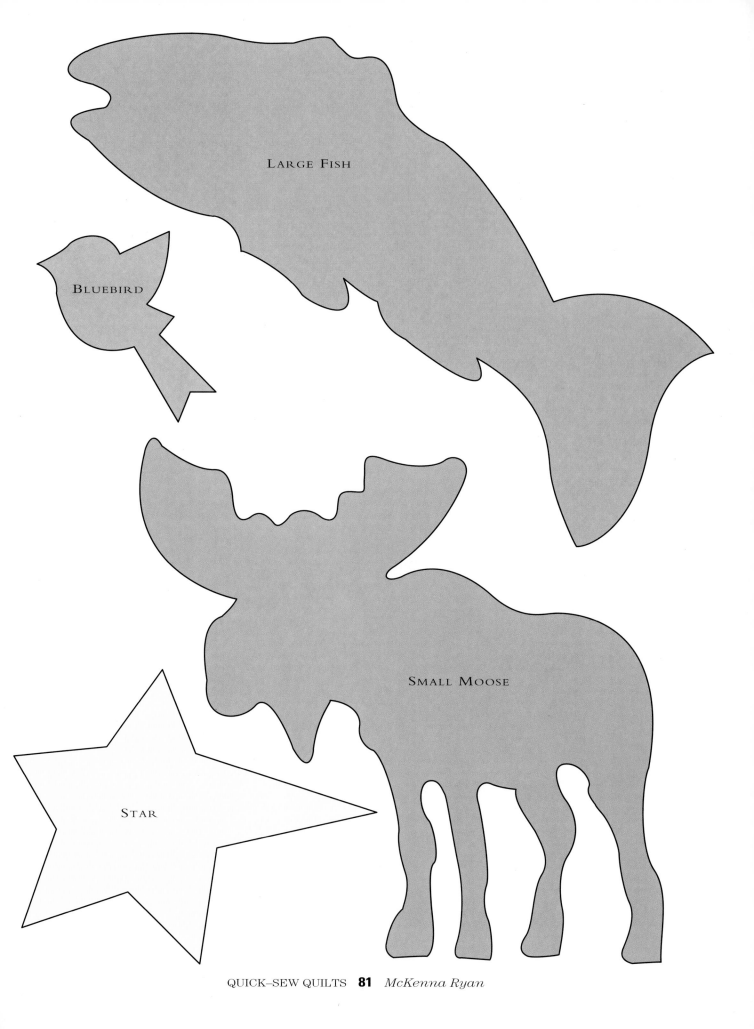

Large Fish

Bluebird

Small Moose

Star

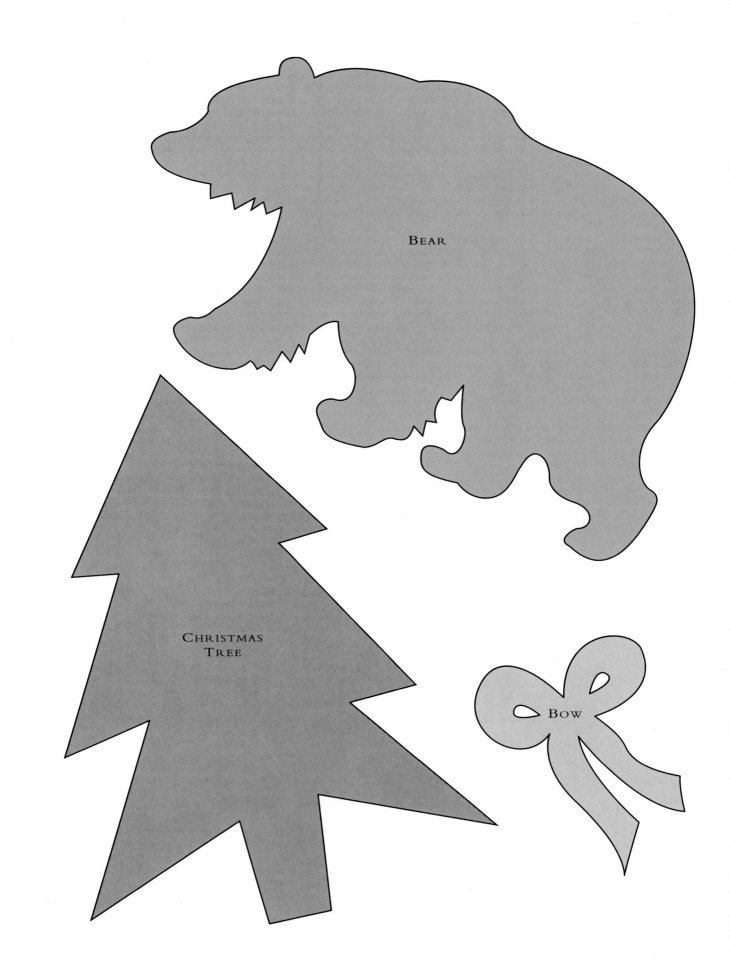

BEAR

CHRISTMAS
TREE

BOW

TIPS & TECHNIQUES

TEA-STAINING FABRIC

- Let eight teabags steep in 3 cups of boiling water until cool. Place the fabric in the tea solution and soak ½ to 3 hours, depending on the desired depth of color.

- To stain a project after sewing and stuffing is completed, apply the tea solution with a cotton ball, rag, or paper towel, making sure to work the solution into the seams.

SEWING-ON BUTTONS

- For a decorative finish, use three strands of embroidery floss to sew buttons onto quilts and projects. Do not knot the end of the floss. Sew down through one button hole to back of quilt and up through second hole. Tie floss tails together into a knot on top of the button. Apply a dot of clear-drying glue on the knot and clip the floss tails.

USING A HOT GLUE GUN

- When shopping for a hot glue gun look for one with a trigger mechanism for dispersing the hot glue, and with dual temperature controls (or purchase two guns).

- Guns come in two sizes: The large size covers large areas quickly; the small size works great on craft projects that require precision placement of glue.

- Low temperature glue (wax sticks) melts at a lower temperature and is easier to work with, but one caution—the heat of outdoors, a sunny window, or a hot attic (where Christmas decorations are stored) can melt the glue, too.

CLEANING EMBELLISHED CLOTHING

- Hand-wash your fused garment, or turn it inside-out and wash with cold water in the washing machine on the delicate cycle. Line-dry or dry flat. If fused pieces start to lift, use an iron to press them back into place. You may need to place a piece of fusible web under the edge to re-adhere.

- Use lightweight fusible web if you will be machine-washing and drying your garment. If the fabric is stretchy, place a tear-away stabilizer on the inside of the garment, under the design area; machine-appliqué around the pieces to secure them to the fabric.

Janet Pittman

FROM MY MOTHER'S GARDEN

Janet Pittman's recipe for success includes more than a dozen years devoted to the styling of gourmet food to be photographed for upscale cookbooks and magazines. Since the artful arrangement of food requires considerable design expertise and imagination, it provided a wonderful outlet for Janet's creativity for many years.

Early in her career, however, Janet had designed a line of period costumes for a specialty pattern company. Later, after taking up quilting as a hobby, Janet's interest in all aspects of the art of sewing blossomed into a full-fledged love-affair with fabric. Janet established her own business, Garden Trellis Designs, which offers her opportunities for designing with either of her specialties—food or fabric.

The wide range of projects designed by Janet Pittman are inspired by her love of gardening, reflected in the wallhanging shown opposite. The fabrics are a lavish blend of watercolor hues reminiscent of Monet's Garden, and for Janet, the iris and clematis are fond reminders of the flowers that could be found blooming in abundance in her mother's garden all summer long. Start with your favorite floral design from Janet's collection, and soon you'll have your own garden of needlework delights to enjoy all year round!

MATERIALS

- ½ yard of light turquoise print fabric for background
- ¼ yard each of medium and medium-dark turquoise, and dark lavender print fabrics for background
- ¼ yard of dark purple print fabric for inside border
- 1 yard of medium green print for border, and iris stems and leaves
- 1⅓ yards of dark blue print fabric for binding and backing
- ¾ yard of light green print fabric for clematis vines and leaves
- Scraps of white, wine, and medium pink fabrics for flowers
- Fusible web
- 36" square of batting
- Green, violet, lavender, gold, and white rayon thread
- Invisible thread for quilting

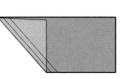

DIAGRAM A

Quick-Sew Wallhanging

Finished size 31" square

CUTTING

1. From the light turquoise print, cut four 5½" squares (A) and four each 2" x 6½" (D), 2" x 8"(E), 2" x 9½" (H) and 2" x 11" (I) strips.

2. From the medium turquoise print, cut four each 2" x 5" (B) and 2" x 6½" (C) strips.

3. From the medium-dark turquoise print, cut four each 2" x 8" (F) and 2" x 9½" (G) strips.

4. From the dark lavender print, cut four each 2" x 11" (J) and 2 x 12½" (K) strips.

5. From the dark purple print, cut four 1½" x 24½" strips.

6. Referring to Diagram A for bias cutting, fold one corner of the light green print at a 45° angle. Cut along this diagonal fold, and then cut four 1½" strips along the diagonal cuts.

7. From the medium green print, cut two 3¾" x 36" strips and two 3¾" x 25" strips. If green print is directional, cut the 36" strips lengthwise, then cut the shorter strips crosswise. Fold and cut the remaining fabric as in Step 6 above to make three 1½" strips for stems.

8. From dark blue print, cut a 34" square for the backing and four 3" x 36" strips for the binding.

9. Refer to the General Instructions on page 6 to trace, apply fusible web to, and cut the following appliqué pieces on pages 92 and 93: Two sets of iris petals 1–5; one iris bud and bud casing; one set of iris leaves A, B and C; six of each clematis petal, two sets of clematis bud and casing, and 27 assorted clematis leaves from the six templates.

PIECING AND APPLIQUÉ

1. Referring to Diagram B, sew four background blocks.

2. Sew the four blocks together with the light turquoise corners in the center.

3. Fold the four dark purple strips in half lengthwise with wrong sides together; press. With one end of a folded strip even with side edge of pieced center, pin strip to top edge of pieced center; sew with a ¼" seam allowance. Cut strip at opposite edge. Leave strip flat against the center. Repeat on the bottom edge. Sew the two remaining folded strips to the side edges of the block.

4. Add the border strips to the pieced center, using Diagram C for reference.

5. Fold the four light green and three medium green bias strips in half lengthwise with wrong sides together; press. Stitch a scant ¼" from the raw edges. Referring to Diagram D, press the strip in half lengthwise with the folded edge covering the raw edge and the stitching. The light green strips are for the clematis vine, and the medium green strips are for the iris stems.

6. Referring to the photograph, arrange

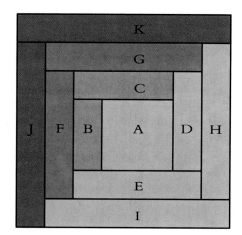

DIAGRAM B

DIAGRAM C

DIAGRAM D

the iris stems, leaves, and then the flowers on the background. Fuse the leaves and the flowers.

7. Sew edges of the stems and leaves with decorative or plain machine-stitching.

8. To make the lacy edge on the iris petals set your machine to a wide zigzag stitch. Drop the feed dogs and proceed as for free-motion stitching. The machine will move the needle from side to side and you will guide the fabric (Diagram E). Make two or three passes over each area to build up the texture.

9. Referring to the photograph, arrange the clematis vine, leaves, stems, and then flowers to the background. Fuse the leaves and flowers. Use decorative or

plain machine-stitching on the edges of the pieces and for veins in the leaves and petals. With a straight stitch and a forward and reverse motion make gold centers.

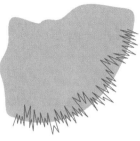

DIAGRAM E

FINISHING

1. Refer to the General Instructions on page 7 to layer, quilt, and bind wallhanging using the 3" dark blue strips and ½" inch seam allowances.

IRIS VEST

Cut out your favorite vest pattern in off-white or other light fabric. Peruse your garden or garden catalogues for colorful varieties of iris, then look through your fabric stash and thread drawer for matching combinations — or make up your own. Cut, position, and fuse the iris pieces to the vest and machine-appliqué as described for the wallhanging. Add a lining and then facings or a binding. For a quick binding, cut 3"-wide bias strips. Fold strips in half with wrong sides together. Cut the raw edges in a wavy pattern or with pinking shears. Trim vest edges to the seam line. Position the folded bias over the edge and stitch down with a couple of rows of free-motion stitching.

Finished size 15" x 39"

MATERIALS

- ⅓ yard of light lavender print fabric for background

- ¼ yard each of medium and medium-dark lavender, and dark purple print fabrics for background

- ¼ yard of turquoise print fabric for border

- ¾ yard of dark turquoise print fabric for binding and backing

- ½ yard of light green print fabric for clematis vines and leaves

- Scraps of bright pink fabrics for flowers

- Fusible web

- Batting

- Green, pink, and gold rayon thread

- Invisible thread for quilting

CUTTING

1. From the light lavender print, cut three 5½" squares (A), and three each 2" x 6½" (D), 2" x 8" (E), 2" x 9½" (H) and 2" x 11" (I) strips.

2. From the medium lavender print, cut three 2" x 5" strips (B) and three 2" x 6½" (C) strips.

3. From the medium-dark lavender print cut three 2" x 8" strips (F) and three 2" x 9½" (G) strips.

4. From the dark purple print, cut three 2" x 11" (J) and three 2" x 12½" (K) strips.

5. From the turquoise print, cut three 2¼" x 44" strips.

6. From the dark turquoise print, cut three 3" x 42" strips and an 18" x 42" rectangle.

7. Referring to Diagram A, page 84, for bias cutting, fold one corner of the light green print at a 45° angle. Cut on the fold, and then cut three 1½" strips along the diagonal cut for vines.

DIAGRAM F

8. Refer to the General Instructions on page 6 to trace, apply fusible web to, and cut the following appliqué pieces on page 92: Six of each clematis petal, two sets of clematis bud and casing, and 15 assorted clematis leaves from the six templates.

PIECING AND APPLIQUÉ

1. Sew three background blocks using Diagram B, page 86, for reference.
2. Referring to the photograph, sew the three blocks together so the colors form a diagonal pattern.
3. Add border strips to the background, using Diagram F for reference.
4. Referring to Diagram D, page 86, fold the three light green bias strips in half lengthwise with wrong sides together; press. Stitch a scant ¼" from the raw edges. Press the strip in half lengthwise with the folded edge covering the raw edge and the stitching.
5. Referring to photograph, arrange the clematis vine, leaves, and then flowers to background. Fuse the leaves and flowers.
6. Use decorative or plain machine-stitching on edges of pieces and for veins in leaves and petals. With a straight stitch make gold centers.

FINISHING

1. Refer to the General Instructions on page 7 to layer, quilt, and bind the wallhanging using the 3" strip and a ½" seam allowance.

Napkin Ring

For 4 Rings

MATERIALS

- 12" square of fuchsia felt
- 12" square of green felt
- Scrap of gold felt
- Fusible web
- Fuchsia, green, and gold rayon thread
- Four green napkin rings

CUTTING

1. Cut fuchsia felt in half. Fuse a 6" x 12" piece of fusible we on one half. Remove the paper backing; fuse the other piece of felt on top.
2. Lightly trace six of each small clematis petal on the felt. Trace two each of the six clematis leaves on a single layer of green felt.
3. Trace four ¾" circles on the gold felt.

STITCHING AND ASSEMBLY

1. Stitch around the traced lines with a decorative machine stitch and the coordinating color of thread. Using two lines of straight stitching, stitch a vein down the center of each petal and leaf.
2. Using a small zigzag stitch and starting in the center, stitch a spiral in each gold circle.

DIAGRAM G

3. Cut out the petals, leaves, and circles, cutting about ¹⁄₁₆" from the outer stitching lines.
4. Referring to Diagram G, hot glue six petals together to form a flower. Cover each center with a gold circle.
5. Hot-glue two leaves to a napkin ring. Hot-glue the third leaf overlapping one of these two; add the flower to the center area.

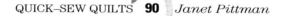

FAST, FUN, AND FABULOUS FLORAL FRAME

Make your favorite photograph more memorable in a floral-bordered frame. Arrange as many blooms and buds as needed to fit the size of your frame.

CLEMATIS CASCADE

Dress up an ordinary white wax candle with a collar of clematis flowers and leaves you can make in minutes from scraps of felt—a dramatic clematis cascade! Let the arrangement take center stage on your dining room table, coordinating it with the napkin ring and table runner.

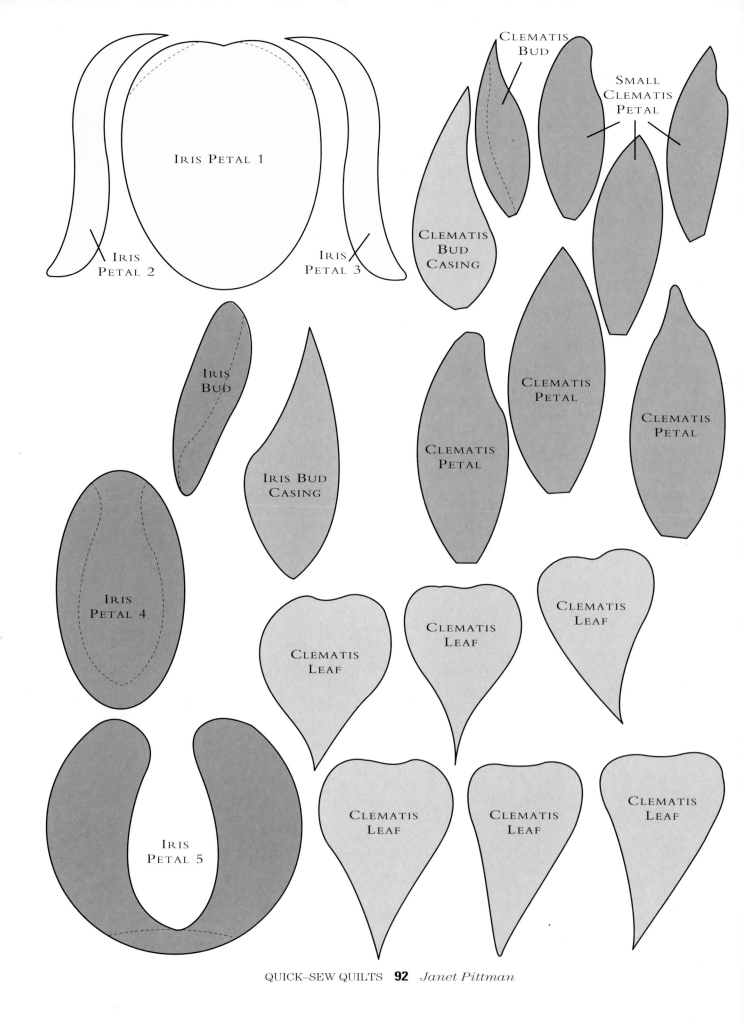

IRIS PETAL 1

IRIS
PETAL 2

IRIS
PETAL 3

CLEMATIS
BUD

SMALL
CLEMATIS
PETAL

CLEMATIS
BUD
CASING

IRIS
BUD

IRIS BUD
CASING

CLEMATIS
PETAL

CLEMATIS
PETAL

CLEMATIS
PETAL

IRIS
PETAL 4

CLEMATIS
LEAF

CLEMATIS
LEAF

CLEMATIS
LEAF

IRIS
PETAL 5

CLEMATIS
LEAF

CLEMATIS
LEAF

CLEMATIS
LEAF

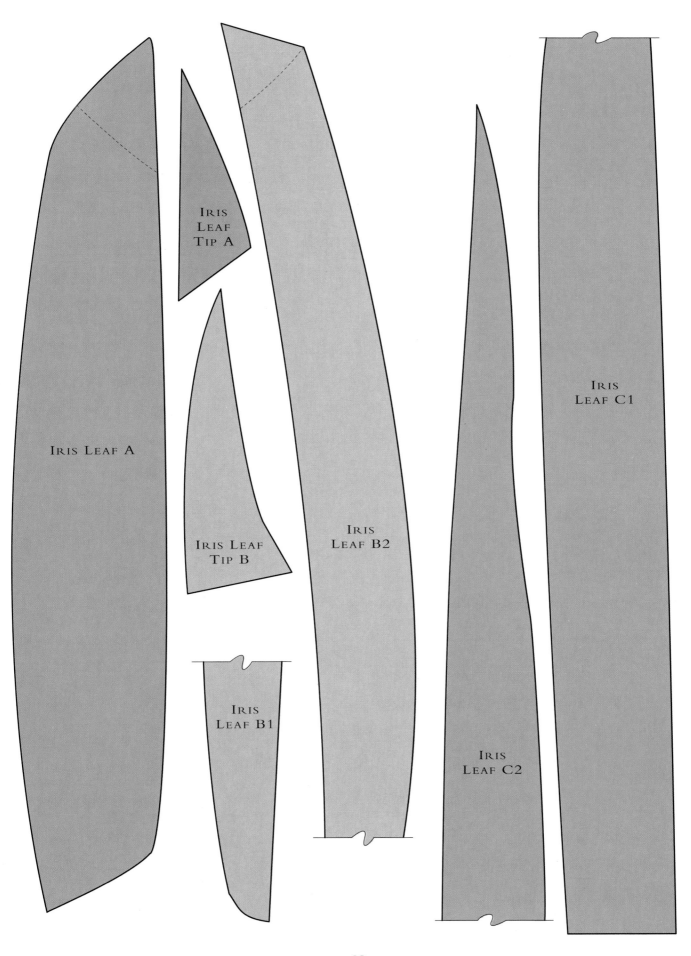

IRIS
LEAF
TIP A

IRIS LEAF A

IRIS LEAF
TIP B

IRIS
LEAF B2

IRIS
LEAF B1

IRIS
LEAF C2

IRIS
LEAF C1

Cheryl Jukich

A s Cheryl Jukich recalls, when she was growing up, there were only two places you needed to look for her—she was either at her mother's sewing machine or in her father's workshop, having the time of her life designing with scraps of fabric or wood.

Since sewing Barbie clothes in the mid-fifties, Cheryl has gathered a wealth of sewing and teaching experience that has taken her from a home-based custom clothing business to a successful pattern and design enterprise.

Her experience as a fabric store clerk and later as a buyer of missy and junior clothing for two major department stores has enabled Cheryl to create patterns that flatter most any figure, require average sewing experience and most importantly, help inspire creativity. Cheryl is president and head designer of The Threadbare Pattern Company, located in Havelock, North Carolina. Her award-winning patterns are recognized for their whimsical 3-D designs and detailed instructions.

As a service to her loyal following of pattern buyers, Cheryl has a help-hotline, named appropriately enough, 1-800-4 PATTERN!

MATERIALS

These quantities are for one panel. Choose a color scheme for each one of the four seasonal panels.

- ¼ yard each of eight fabrics for log cabin squares
- ¼ yard each of five neutral fabrics for fence rail squares
- ¼ yard of osnaburg or muslin for three background squares
- ⅛ yard of two fabrics (one light and one dark) for checkerboard strip
- ½ yard of fabric for sashing and borders
- 25" x 36" piece of cotton batting
- 25" x 36" piece of muslin for backing
- Leftover fabrics from log cabin squares for appliqué pieces
- One ball of medium jute twine for arms, legs, and trim
- Fusible web
- Gold and beige thread
- Six 1" wooden buttons
- Eighteen ½" wooden buttons
- Three month-of-year porcelain buttons
- Three porcelain buttons to coordinate with month buttons
- Three "primitive people" porcelain buttons for faces

Quick-Sew Wallhanging
Finished size 30" x 44"

CUTTING

1. From each log cabin fabric and fence rail fabric, cut one 1½" strip across width of fabric.

2. From each checkerboard fabric, cut one 1½" strip.

3. From background fabric, cut three 8½" squares.

4. From the border fabric, cut two 1½" x 8½" sashing strips and three 2½" x 44" strips.

5. Refer to the General Instructions on page 6 to trace, apply fusible web to, and cut the following appliqué pieces on page 104: Three dresses, three bloomers, and one apron.

6. From twine, cut three 12" lengths for arms and six 5" lengths for legs.

7. From log cabin fabrics, cut eighteen ½" x 7" strips for hair and feet.

8. From border fabrics, cut three 2½" x 13" strips; from three log cabin strips, cut one each 2½" x 13" strip for hanging tabs.

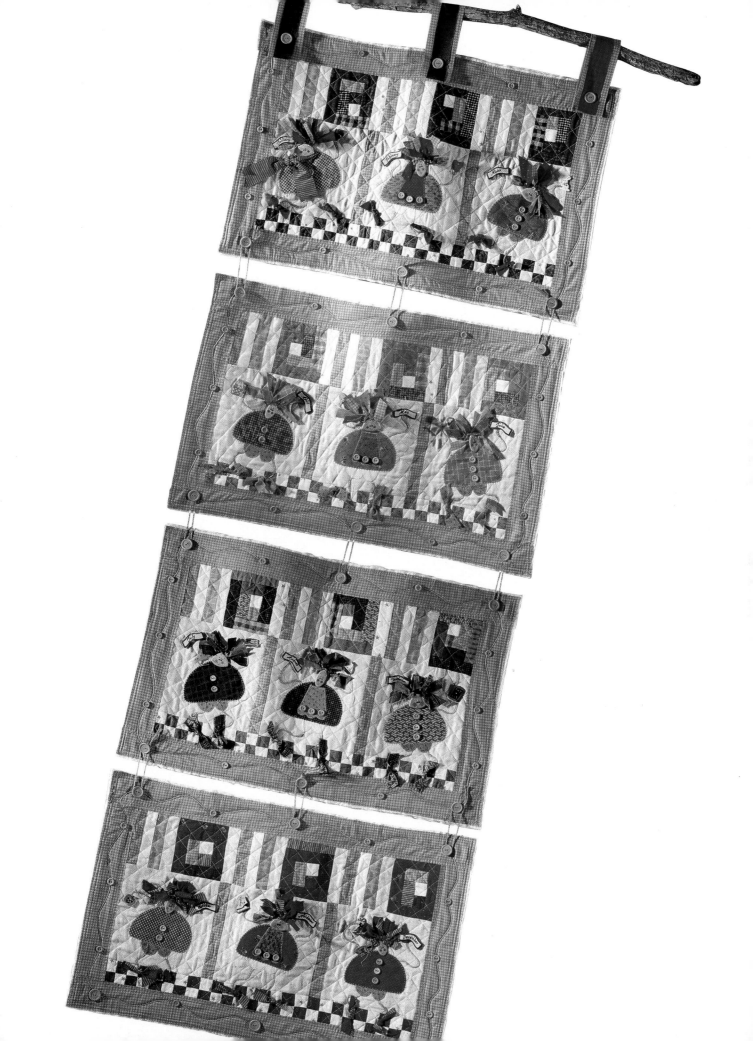

PIECING

1. Referring to Diagram A and following the directions below, make three log cabin blocks.

2. From a light colored strip, cut three 1½" center squares.

3. With right sides together, sew the center square to a strip of fabric. Remove from machine and cut strip even with center square. Set leftover strip aside. Open just-sewn square; finger press.

4. Choose another color strip and sew with right sides together to the two squares. Cut strip even with squares. Set leftover strip aside.

5. Continue adding strips in this manner, setting aside leftover strips for use in the next block. Each block should measure approximately 4½" x 5½".

6. Arrange four fence rail strips in a pleasing manner. Sew long edges of strips with right sides together. Press seam allowances to one side.

7. From the fence rail unit, cut three 5½" blocks. Set the remainder of the unit aside for the other panels.

8. With right sides together, sew one log cabin block to a fence rail block along the 5½" edges as shown in Diagram B. Repeat with remaining log cabin and fence rail blocks; press.

9. Cut two 5½" pieces from the remaining fence rail strip. Sew one each to the fence rail side of a log cabin/fence rail unit as shown in Diagram C. Repeat for one additional unit (two units now have five rails and one has four).

10. Stitch the 3 units together referring to Diagram C; press. This is the fence rail/log cabin unit.

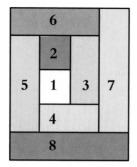

DIAGRAM A

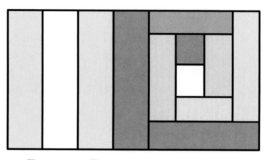

DIAGRAM B

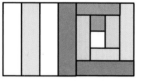  

DIAGRAM C

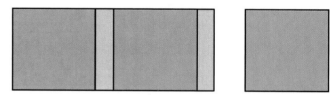

DIAGRAM D

11. Referring to Diagram D, sew an 8½" sashing strip to each side edge of one background square; add the remaining background squares to each side of this unit; press. This is the background unit.

12. For the checkerboard, sew one dark strip and one light strip with right sides together. Press the seam allowances toward the dark strip. Referring to Diagram E, cut the strip into twenty six 1½" units.

13. Referring to Diagram F, place two units with right sides together, forming a checkerboard pattern. Continue adding all units, forming a checkerboard strip.

14. With right sides together, sew the fence rail/log cabin strip to the top of the background unit; sew the checkerboard strip to the bottom.

15. Lay batting on a flat surface. Center the pieced background on the batting. Stitch ¼" from the outer edge of the fabric. Mark diagonal quilting lines 1" apart on background; machine-quilt.

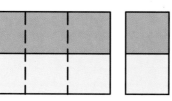

DIAGRAM E

DIAGRAM F

16. Referring to Diagram G, arrange one dress, bloomers, and apron on center background square. Center arm twine behind shoulder area and a twine leg under each side of bloomers; fuse fabric pieces in place. Sew around pieces with a decorative stitch. Repeat in the other two squares, omitting the apron.

17. Position the twine arms outward and upward. Zigzag loosely over the arms. Cut away the excess twine. Repeat for legs, letting them wander onto checkerboard area.

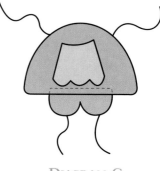

DIAGRAM G

FINISHING

1. Cut one border strip in half crosswise. Referring to Diagram H, place one half on either side of pieced center with a ½" overlap; stitch in place with a decorative machine stitch. Sew remaining two strips to top and bottom edges of pieced center. Leave the edges untrimmed.

2. Lay muslin backing on a flat surface. Center pieced top and batting on backing. Sew through all layers, ¼" from the outside edges of the border.

3. Very casually, trim away excess backing and batting up to the border edges, keeping it primitive looking. Edges will be uneven with bits of batting showing.

4. Find the center of the top and bottom borders, mark button placement with an X. Mark corner buttons 2¼" from the edges (Diagram I). These six buttons are the hanging buttons and must be spaced the same on all four panels.

5. Draw a curvy line inside border, passing through each X. Loosely zigzag twine onto borders using the line as a guide.

6. Sew a 1" wooden button at each X, referring to Step 10 for top unit. Sew ten smaller wooden buttons evenly spaced in the border.

7. Referring to the photograph on page 97 for placement, sew the remaining wooden buttons to the dresses, and sew the month and seasonal theme porcelain buttons to the end of each arm.

8. For feet, place two different-color ½" x 7" strips wrong sides together. Sew center of strips to end of each leg to make feet. Tie each foot in a knot. Trim ends to 1".

9. For hair, place two different-color ½" x 7" strips wrong sides together. Fold in half. Place fold behind hole in button face. Tack strips to head (Diagram J); repeat for remaining two

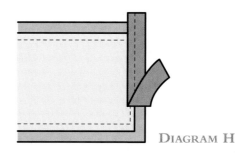

DIAGRAM H

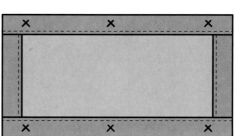

DIAGRAM I

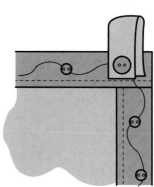

DIAGRAM K

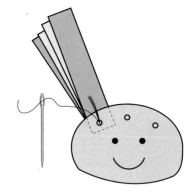

DIAGRAM J

holes. Tie hair into knots to make it pouf. Trim. Stitch each button face to top of dress. If desired, add a strip of fabric for a scarf to one of the winter dolls.

10. For the hanging tabs, place one 13" log cabin strip on top of each 13" border fabric strip. Fold in half; pin to top border at the X marks. Sew on the large wooden buttons, securing the tabs to the panel (Diagram K).

11. For twine hangers to attach lower panels, cut three 14" lengths of twine. Fold in half and tie a knot so the loop is 4½" long.

12. Use a gnarly branch or ¾" dowel for a hanging rod.

Pillow
21" pillow

MATERIALS

- Large scraps of light and medium brown, green, gold, white, and off-white fabric for appliqué
- 15½" square of osnaburg or muslin for background
- ¼ yard of ten different fabrics for log cabin and fence rail blocks and borders
- ¾ yard of fabric for ruffle
- ¾ yard of osnaburg or muslin for pillow back
- Fusible web
- One ball of medium jute twine
- Gold and beige thread
- One "primitive people" button for face
- One each seed packet, garden spade, watermelon slice, and blackbird porcelain button, and two each carrot, turnip, and corn porcelain buttons
- 20" pillow form
- Nine ½" wooden buttons

CUTTING

1. Refer to the General Instructions on page 6 to trace, apply fusible web to, and cut the following appliqué pieces on pages 104–105: One each dress, bloomers, sun, and "Farm Fresh" sign.
2. From light brown fabric, cut two 1¾" x 5½" strips. From medium brown fabric, cut two 1¼" x 5½" strips.
3. From twine, cut a 12" length for arms and two 4" lengths for legs.
4. From off-white fabric, cut two ⅜" x 1¾" strips and one 3" x 4½" rectangle for apron.

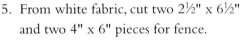

5. From white fabric, cut two 2½" x 6½" and two 4" x 6" pieces for fence.
6. From log cabin, fence rail, and border fabrics, cut two 1½" strips across the width of the fabric.
7. From ruffle fabric, cut four 6½" x 21½" rectangles.
8. From pillow back fabric, cut two 21½" x 24½" rectangles.

PIECING

1. With right sides together and alternating colors, stitch light and medium brown strips together to form garden plot. Referring to the photograph above, position garden plot on the background; sew in place.
2. Fuse sun to upper right corner, and stitch. Satin-stitch squiggly sun rays.
3. Referring to the photograph and Diagram G, page 97, position bloomers, dress, and twine for arms and legs; fuse. Fuse apron straps in place.

4. Fold the large piece of off-white fabric in half lengthwise. Stitch as shown in Diagram L, leaving an opening to turn. Clip corners and turn; press. Place over apron straps, overlapping about ¼". Sew along side and bottom edges; stitch across to form three pockets (Diagram M).

DIAGRAM L

5. Using the permanent marker, print the words Farm Fresh on the sign; fuse in place. Sew around sign.

6. For fence rails, fold narrow fence strips in half lengthwise. Sew open edges closed, leaving an opening to turn. Clip corners, turn, and press. Trace fence post pattern twice to wrong side of one large piece of fence fabric. Place the other piece under it. Sew on traced lines, leaving opening to turn. Cut ¼" beyond stitching lines. Clip corners, turn, and press.

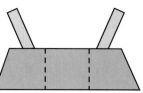

DIAGRAM M

7. Sew fence rails in lower right corner. Sew down pickets with diagonal lines where they cross rails.

8. Following Steps 1–6 of Piecing the Wallhanging on page 96, make two log cabin blocks, adding a ninth strip to each block, and one fence rail block from five 5½" long fence rail strips.

9. With right sides together, stitch log cabin blocks to opposite sides of the fence rail block. Sew unit to the top of the appliquéd background. Sew a border strip to the bottom of the background; trim edges even.

10. Following Steps 12 and 13 on page 97, make a checkerboard strip; sew to right side of background. Sew a border strip to right side of checkerboard strip.

11. Sew three border strips to the left side of the background.

FINISHING

1. Wind twine 3–4 times around a 3" piece of cardboard. Slip off twine and fold in half. Repeat two more times. Sew twine bunches randomly across garden plot for weeds. Cut tops of loops (Diagram N).

2. Referring to Step 9 on page 98, add hair to the face button. Sew button in place. Sew veggie buttons to garden plot, blackbird button to top of sign, and a wooden button at the neck of the dress. Slip the seed packet and spade buttons into apron pockets; sew in place.

3. Fold ruffle strips in half lengthwise with right sides together. Sew short ends. Clip corners and turn. Press.

4. Stitch strips to top and bottom edges of pillow top, leaving ¼" of the pillow top exposed at each end (Diagram O). Repeat on the side edges.

5. Fold the backing rectangles in half with wrong sides together, forming two 12¼" x 21½" rectangles. Proceed as directed for Pine Tree Pillow, steps 12 and 13 on page 12.

6. Turn right side out. Fold down each corner of the ruffle and secure with a wooden button.

7. Insert pillow form.

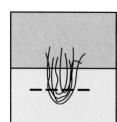

DIAGRAM N

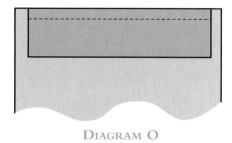

DIAGRAM O

FOR A LITTLE SLICE OF FUN— DECORATE A SHIRT

Choose your favorite doll design from those shown on the wallhanging. Cut out and apply fusible web to a dress appliqué; position inside the shirt pocket. Add twine arms. Fuse and stitch the dress. Bring twine arms together over top; stitch in place. Add cotton-yarn doll hair to face button and tack to top of dress. Sew a watermelon slice button above the doll's head and two more buttons to the collar. If desired, replace shirt buttons with watermelon-seed buttons.

CHATTY BLOOMERS' FRIENDSHIP GARDEN— DECORATE A COLLAR

Have fun personalizing the techniques used in this chapter's three projects. The ladies in their bloomers are having tea across the back fence. One lady could have fabric-strip hair instead of cotton-yarn doll hair. Add yo-yo flowers from page 14, using decorative buttons for the centers. Tack all kinds of porcelain buttons to the collar. Then, add a large bow to the front in a complementary fabric.

MATERIALS

- 2 yards of blue chambray for front and lining of your favorite vest pattern

- Large scraps of red-and-gold print, brown check, red-and-beige stripe, beige solid, and green knit fabric for appliqué

- 1 to 1½ yards of thin batting

- Gold and beige thread

- Cotton-yarn doll hair

- Fusible web

- One ball of medium jute twine

- Six ⅝" hook-and-loop dot sets

- Two "primitive people" face buttons

- Twelve 1" wooden, two small beige, and six small black buttons

- Six skate, two mitten, and four gold star porcelain buttons

- Permanent marker

CUTTING

1. Refer to the General Instructions on page 6 to trace, apply fusible web to, and cut the following appliqué pieces on pages 104–107: One dress, small dress, long-johns, small long-johns, moon, Beware! Thin Ice! sign and sign post, skate shack shelf and roof, pond, snow drifts 1 and 2, Moonlight Skating Tonight sign, and two skate shack uprights and signs.

2. From the red-and-beige stripe fabric, cut twelve ½" x 5" strips for shoulder loops, and three 1¼" x 7" strips for scarves.

3. Using vest pattern, cut out two vest fronts and one back each from chambray, lining, and thin batting, adding 1" to the side seams.

4. From twine, cut six 6" lengths for legs, and three 12" pieces for arms.

5. From brown check, cut two ½" x 6" strips for skate laces.

APPLIQUÉ

1. With right sides up, layer chambray vest fronts on top of batting vest fronts, sew or serge about ¼" from edges.

2. Referring to the photograph and Diagram G on page 97, position the small dress in lower center of left vest front; position small long-johns and twine arms and legs under dress; fuse, and sew with decorative stitches. Arrange arms and legs; zigzag in place.

3. Arrange the skate shack uprights, roof, and shelf around and over skater; fuse and sew. Fuse and sew a snow drift at the foot of each upright.

4. Using a permanent marker, print the words on the signs. Arrange the small signs on the uprights and the skating sign on the roof; fuse and sew.

5. Position the moon about 3" below the shoulder seam. Position twine arms and legs under moon (Diagram P); fuse and sew. Arrange arms upward and outward and legs down; zigzag in place.

6. Position the dress and long-johns on the right vest front. Position twine arms and legs; fuse and sew. Arrange arms and legs; zigzag in place.

7. Position sign pole, sign, and pond near second skater; fuse and sew.

DIAGRAM P

FINISHING

1. With right sides together, place each vest front on a lining piece. Stitch around the fronts using the pattern's recommended seam allowance, leaving an opening in the side seam for turning. Clip corners and curves. Turn and press.

2. Layer the back batting and back; machine-quilt in a 1" diagonal grid pattern. Place back right side up. With raw edges even, pin three pairs of ties on each shoulder, placing one pair about ¼" from each end and one pair in center.

3. Place lining on back with right sides together. Sew around the back using the pattern's seam allowance, leaving an opening in one side seam. Clip corners and curves. Turn and press.

4. Sew three wooden buttons on each front shoulder, evenly spaced opposite the ties on the back shoulders.

5. On the outside of the vest back, place a hook or loop dot in the center and at top and bottom of each side seam; sew in place. Mark corresponding placement on the inside of the vest fronts; sew corresponding dots in place, sewing wooden buttons to the outside of the vest fronts at the same time.

6. Tack the center of a scarf strip to the neck area of each skater and about 1½" from the top of the moon. Tie each scarf in a knot; trim ends in an inverted V.

7. Wrap cotton-yarn hair six times around a 2" piece of cardboard; remove. Repeat five more times. Tack three bundles above each face button for wild hair. Tack the faces to the skaters.

8. Sew the black buttons to ends of skaters' legs for feet and to end of moon's arms for hands. Sew small beige buttons on dress, mitten buttons to ends of skaters' arms, and skate buttons to ends of moon's legs.

9. Cut ends of skate-lace strips in inverted V shape. Fold strip almost in half and tack to bottom of Skates $1.00 sign, and to left arm of skater. Twist strips; secure each end with a skate button.

10. Sew a star button at the top of the Moonlight Skating sign, and sew the remaining star buttons scattered on the right side.

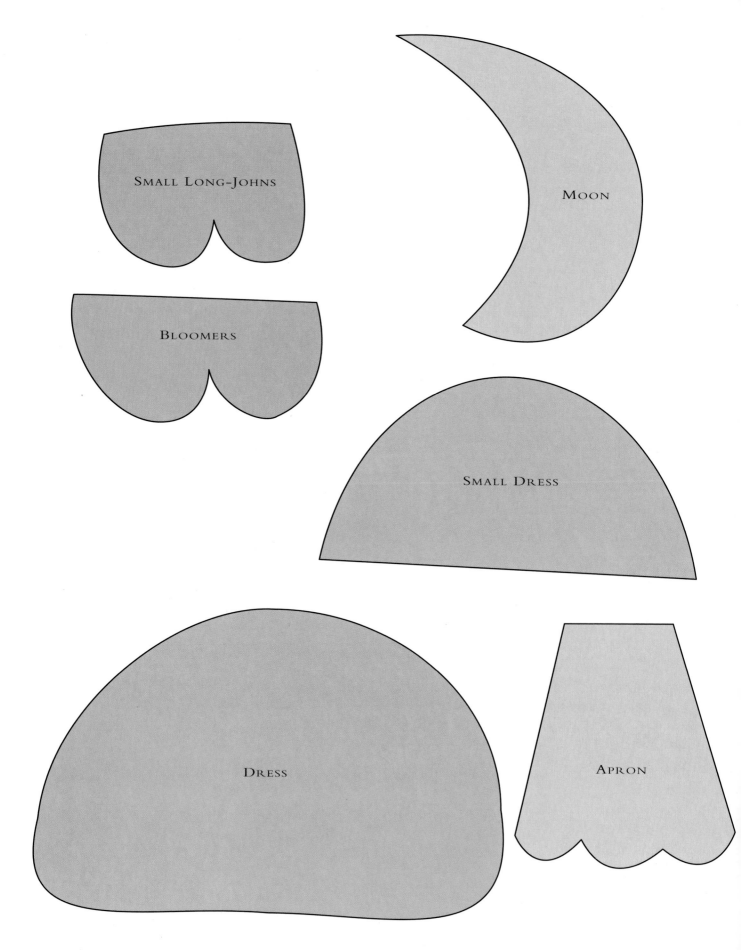

SMALL LONG-JOHNS

MOON

BLOOMERS

SMALL DRESS

DRESS

APRON

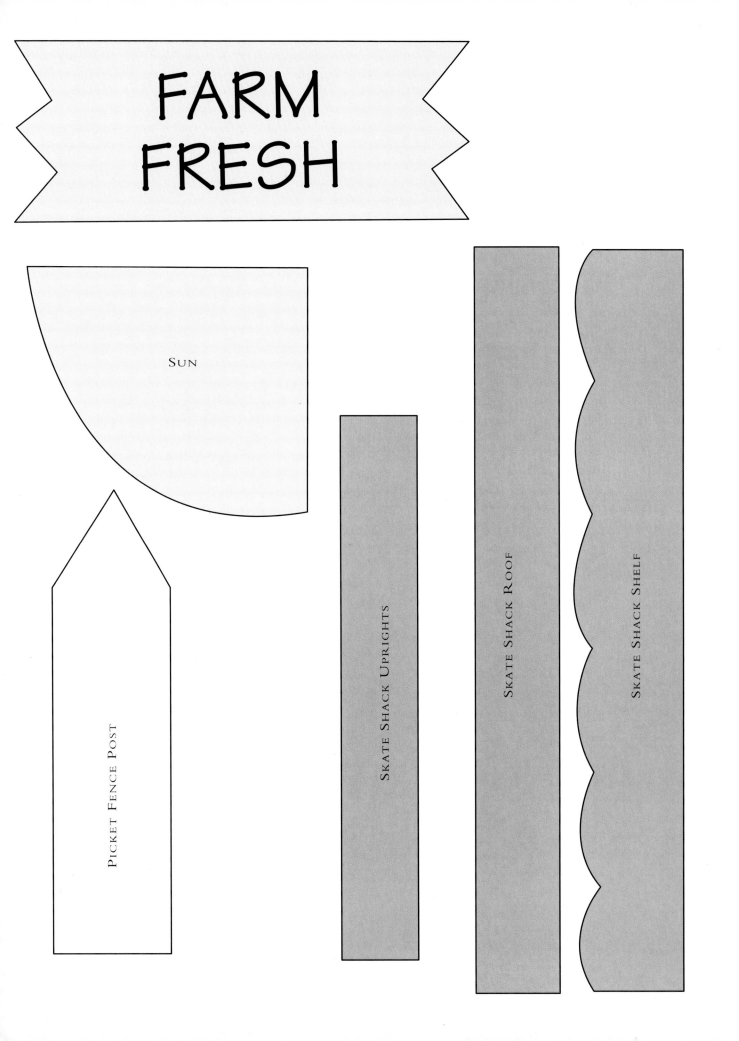

FARM
FRESH

Sun

Picket Fence Post

Skate Shack Uprights

Skate Shack Roof

Skate Shack Shelf

SNOW DRIFT 1

SNOW DRIFT 2

LONG-JOHNS

MOONLIGHT
SKATING
TONIGHT 7PM

SIGN

FROZEN POND

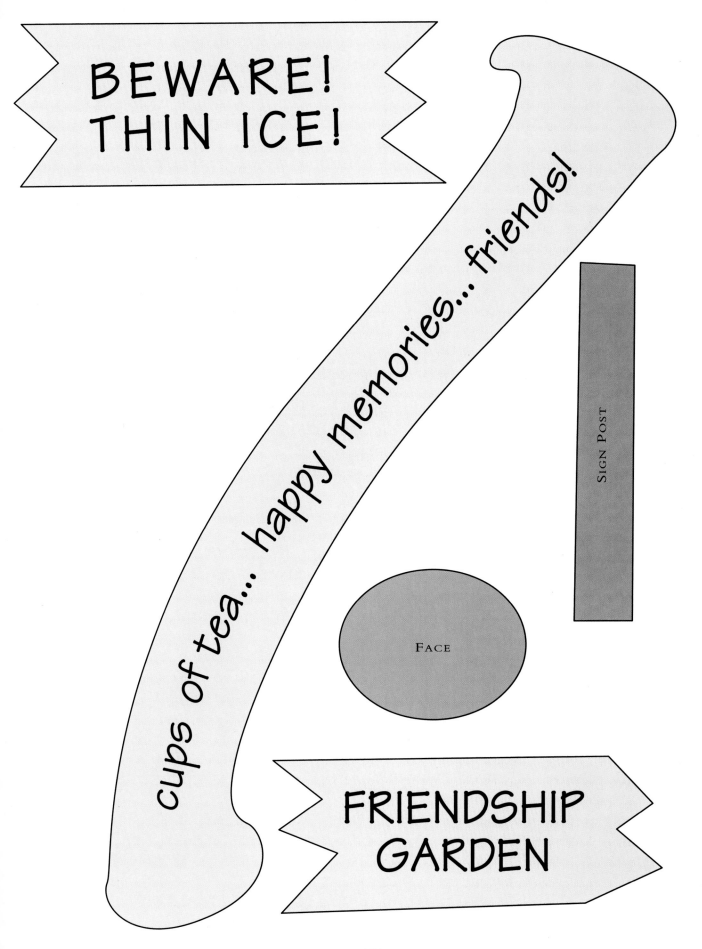

BEWARE!
THIN ICE!

cups of tea... happy memories... friends!

Sign Post

Face

FRIENDSHIP
GARDEN

Kris Kerrigan

In 1993, Kris Kerrigan's interest in quilting expanded into a full-blown business following a simple request from well-known quilting expert Liz Porter, who approached Kris about using Kris' unique design talents to produce patterns to showcase a new line of fabrics.

Since that time, Kris has developed an ever-expanding collection of patterns, featuring chickens, cows, pigs, barns, fences, and other farm-inspired motifs in her Button Weeds Pattern Company. Kris Kerrigan's chickens have become a favorite design motif—truly "something to crow about!"

As a busy farm wife, business woman, and mother of two boys and two girls, Kris places priority in using simple rotary-cut pieces for most of the design motifs in her collection, like the triangles used for the chickens. Quick-fusing appliqué techniques easily polish off with embroidered blanket stitches. When you begin making projects from the kitchen collection shown here, you'll also discover that Kris' rural roots have influenced another aspect of her designs. They are bright, fun, quick, and easy—but practical as well. You'll find everything from a clever cornice board for a window, to a four-slice toaster cover—just right for that hearty breakfast on the farm!

MATERIALS

- 1 yard of black check fabric for border and back
- ⅓ yard each of black plaid, red plaid, and green check fabrics for backgrounds
- ¼ yard of light brown or tan stripe fabrics for borders
- ⅛ yard each of black print, red print, green plaid, gold print, gold check, tan print, and two more light brown or tan stripe fabrics for appliqué
- Scrap of muslin
- Checkered Border, see page 110
- ½ yard of lightweight fusible web
- 21" x 40" piece of batting
- Six ⅜" black buttons
- Three ¼" black buttons
- Gold and ecru embroidery floss
- Gold, ecru, red, and black thread

Quick–Sew Wallhanging

Approximately 20" x 39"

CUTTING

1. From the black check fabric, cut a 21" x 40" rectangle for the back, and two each 3½" x 14" strips and 3½" x 39" strips for the borders.

2. From the black plaid, red plaid, and green check cut one 10" x 12" rectangle each for backgrounds.

3. From the first light brown or tan stripe fabric cut four 1½" x 12" strips and two 1½" x 33" strips for the sashing. From the second light brown or tan stripe fabric, cut a 3½" x 6" rectangle and rip into twelve ½" x 3½" pieces for straw.

4. Refer to the General Instructions on page 6 to trace, apply fusible web to, and cut the following appliqué pieces: From the black print cut a ¾" x 12" strip for loft, a ½" x 8½" strip for ladder, six ½" x 2" strips for ladder rungs, and a 2" x 5" rectangle for nest. From the red print fabric, cut two 2½" squares for the rooster combs/wattles, and two 2" squares for the hen combs/wattles.

5. From the green plaid fabric, cut tall corn stalk and medium corn stalk using the patterns on pages 116–117.

6. From the gold print fabric, cut two 4" squares for roosters and two 1½" squares for hen wings and chick.

7. From the gold check fabric, cut two 3" squares for hens, two 2" squares for rooster wings, and a 1½" square for two chicks.

8. From the tan print fabric, cut a 4½" circle for moon.

9. From the third light brown or tan stripe fabric cut two ¾" x 7½" strips for fence rails and three ¾" x 3" strips for fence posts.

10. From a muslin scrap, cut three eggs.

11. Cut all red print, gold print, and gold check in squares half diagonally to form triangles.

12. Cut three 1½" strips across Checkered Border fabric.

1. Fuse appliqué pieces to background rectangles, referring to photograph on page 109 and the directions that follow. Machine appliqué at the step directed. Refer to the Stitch Guide on page 29 for machine-appliqué stitch ideas.

2. Center and fuse all rooster and hen wings on their bodies.

3. Place rooster comb/wattle, rooster body, hen comb/wattle, and hen body on the black plaid background; fuse and appliqué.

4. Fuse loft strip 1¼" from top edge of red plaid background. Fuse the ladder rungs ⅝" apart on left side. Fuse the ladder side pieces, slightly overlapping edges of rungs; appliqué.

5. Fuse the nest in the right bottom corner of the red plaid background. Tack five ripped pieces of straw on nest.

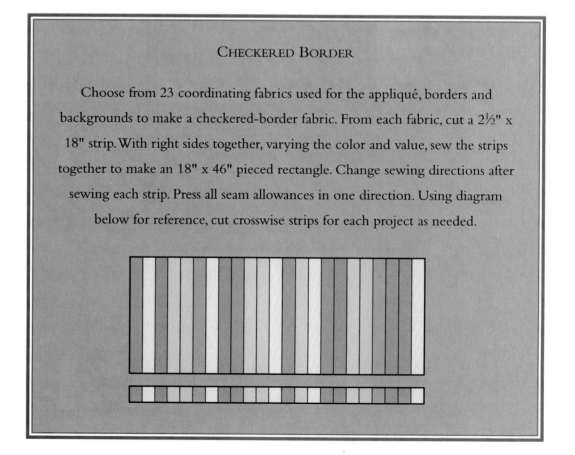

CHECKERED BORDER

Choose from 23 coordinating fabrics used for the appliqué, borders and backgrounds to make a checkered-border fabric. From each fabric, cut a 2½" x 18" strip. With right sides together, varying the color and value, sew the strips together to make an 18" x 46" pieced rectangle. Change sewing directions after sewing each strip. Press all seam allowances in one direction. Using diagram below for reference, cut crosswise strips for each project as needed.

and seven pieces on the loft. Fuse hen's comb/wattle and body by nest. Fuse eggs on nest. Fuse rooster's comb/wattle and body by ladder; appliqué.

6. Fuse hen comb/wattle and body and chicks to green check background with the bodies' bottom points 1¼" from lower edge of background. Fuse rooster 3⅛" above second chick; appliqué.

7. Sew a ¼" button on each chick for an eye, and a ⅜" button on each hen and rooster for an eye.

8. Embroider gold rooster tail feathers in stem stitch, and hen tail feathers, all legs, and toes in long stitch.

9. Sew the quilt top together using Diagram A for reference.

10. Fuse the moon and all but the top 1" of the short corn stalk to the upper right corner; appliqué. Cut two 2½" pieces of ecru embroidery floss for tassels. Fold each piece in half, and lay folded end under the top of the stalk. Sew back and forth across the fold. See Diagram B.

11. Fuse the top of the stalk. Repeat this process for the tall stalk in the bottom left corner. Appliqué the two stalks.

12. Fuse the fence rails and posts on the green plaid block and into the border, with the top of the left post supporting the rooster; appliqué.

FINISHING

1. Refer to the General Instructions on page 7 to layer the wallhanging.

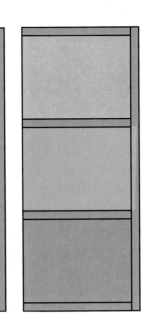
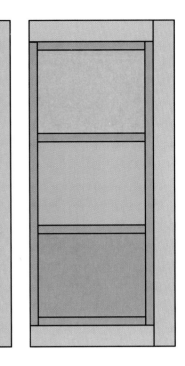

DIAGRAM A

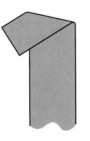

DIAGRAM B

2. Using a long running stitch and black thread, quilt around all chicken bodies, the fence, the corn stalks, at the borders, and around the moon. Use quilt stitches to create slats for the barn and sound waves for the bottom rooster. Use two strands of gold floss to stitch double-cross stars in the sky.

3. Sew Checkered Border strips together lengthwise to form binding. Refer to the General Instructions on page 7 to bind your wallhanging.

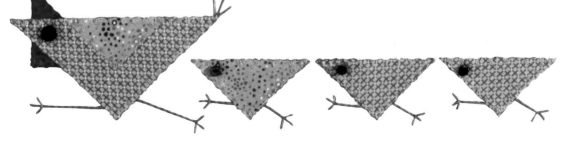

Cornice Board

For a 32" to 34" window

MATERIALS

- ⅓ yard of black check fabric
- Checkered Border, see page 110
- Large scraps of red print, light stripe, gold print, gold check, and orange print fabrics
- ⅛ yard of green plaid fabric
- Gold and ecru embroidery floss
- Gold, ecru, red, and black thread
- Three ¼" black buttons
- Two ⅜" buttons
- 12" x 44" piece of fusible fleece
- 12" x 44" piece of foam core board. NOTE: If window is narrower or wider than 34", adjust the 44" length of the foam core board, referring to Diagram C.

CUTTING

1. From black check fabric, cut a 12" x 44" rectangle for background.

2. Cut one 3½" strip across Checkered Border fabric.

3. Refer to the General Instructions on page 6 to trace, apply fusible web to, and cut the following appliqué pieces:

4. From the light stripe fabric, cut two 1" x 14" strips for fence rails and four 1" x 4½" strips for fence posts.

5. From the red print fabric, cut a 2½" square for rooster comb/wattle and a 1¾" square for comb/wattle.

6. From gold print fabric, cut a 4½" square for rooster body, a 1¾" square for hen wing, and a 2" square for one chick.

7. From gold check, cut a 3½" square for hen body, a 2¼" square for rooster wing, and a 2" square for two chicks.

8. From orange print fabric cut a 4½" circle for the sun.

9. From green plaid fabric, cut three short corn stalks, using pattern on page 117.

10. Cut all red print, gold print and gold check squares in half diagonally to form triangles.

APPLIQUÉ AND ASSEMBLY

1. With right sides together, sew the Checkered Border strip to a long side of the background. For a hem, turn under ¼" and stitch all edges.

2. Fuse appliqué pieces to black check background, referring to the photograph below and the directions that follow. Machine-appliqué at the step directed.

3. Fuse the fence rails and posts to the left side, spacing the rails 1" and posts 1½" from the ends and 2½" apart; machine-appliqué.

4. Center and fuse rooster and hen wings to body.

5. Fuse the rooster comb/wattle and body/wing, resting the body on the left post. Fuse the hen comb/wattle and body/wing and chicks ½" from top of border; machine-appliqué.

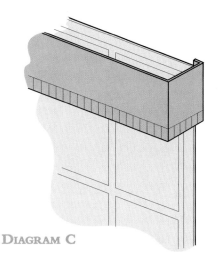

DIAGRAM C

6. Fuse the sun, centering 11" from left side and 7½" above the Checkered Border; appliqué.

7. Fuse and tassel the corn stalks as in Steps 10 and 11 on page 111.

8. Stem-stitch the rooster's tail feathers in gold floss. Long-stitch the legs, toes, and hen's tail feathers in gold, also. Use black thread to long-stitch three sound waves from the rooster's beak. Sew ¼" buttons for chick eyes and ⅜" buttons for the hen and rooster eyes.

9. Fuse the fusible fleece to the back of the cornice board cover so the Checkered Border front will be 2" deep. (The remaining depth will be glued to the back of the board.)

10. Use a crafts knife to score the top cardboard and foam layers of the foam core board at 1" and 5" from each end. Do not cut through to the bottom cardboard; if you do, tape it back together. Fold back at each score line.

11. Place the cover on the board. Fold back the top and bottom hems and glue to the back side of the board, easing the fabric over the board folds. Refer to Diagram C. The 1" fold is the edge to be nailed to the window frame and the 4" extension provides the cornice board's depth.

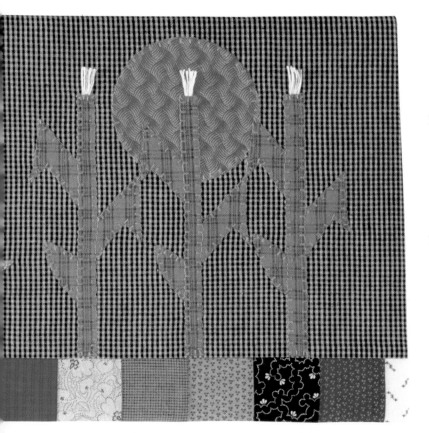

Towel

Approximately 17" x 31"

MATERIALS

- ½ yard of black check for towel
- ⅛ yard of green check for towel band
- Scraps of red print, gold print, and gold check fabrics
- Checkered Border, see page 110
- Gold embroidery floss
- Gold, red, and black thread
- Three ¼" black buttons
- One ⅜" black button

CUTTING

1. From the green check fabric cut a 4½" x 18" rectangle for towel band.
2. Refer to the General Instructions on page 6 to trace, apply fusible web to, and cut the following appliqué pieces:
3. From red print fabric, cut a 1¾" square for hen comb/wattle.
4. From gold print fabric, cut a 1½" square for hen wing and one chick.
5. From gold check fabric cut a 3" square for hen body and a 1½" square for two chicks.
6. Cut all red print, gold print, and gold check squares in half diagonally to form triangles.
7. Cut two 1¾" x 18" strips across the Checkered Border fabric.
8. From the black check fabric, cut an 18" x 32" rectangle for the towel.

APPLIQUÉ AND ASSEMBLY

1. Fuse appliqué pieces to green check rectangle. Machine-appliqué at the step directed.

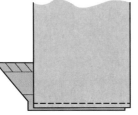

DIAGRAM F

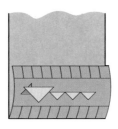

DIAGRAM G

2. Center and fuse wing to hen body. Fuse and appliqué hen comb/wattle, hen wing/body, and three chicks centered on green check band.
3. Sew Checkered Border strips to top and bottom edges of green band. Press seam allowances toward band. Press under a ¼" hem at the top edge of the band.
4. Long-stitch hen tail feathers and all legs and toes with gold floss.
5. Sew three ¼" buttons for chick eyes and the ⅜" button for hen eye.
6. Refer to Diagrams F and G: With bottom edges matching, place right side of band to wrong side of towel; sew bottom edges together. Flip and press band to front of towel. Using a running stitch and black quilting thread, sew top edge of band to towel.
7. Press under ¼" on side edges of towel, press under ¼" again and machine-hem. Repeat for top edge of towel. Decorate bottom and side edges of band using a running stitch and black quilting thread.

Pot Holder

9" square

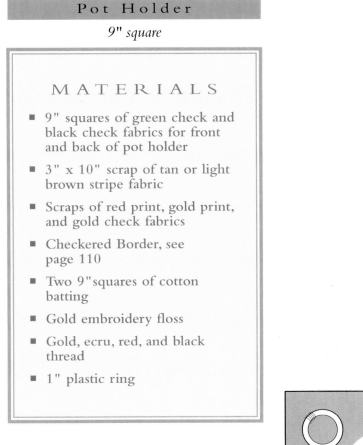

MATERIALS

- 9" squares of green check and black check fabrics for front and back of pot holder
- 3" x 10" scrap of tan or light brown stripe fabric
- Scraps of red print, gold print, and gold check fabrics
- Checkered Border, see page 110
- Two 9" squares of cotton batting
- Gold embroidery floss
- Gold, ecru, red, and black thread
- 1" plastic ring

CUTTING GUIDE

1. Refer to the General Instructions on page 7 to apply fusible web to, and cut the following appliqué pieces:
2. From tan or light brown stripe, cut a ¾" x 10" strip for top fence rail, a ¾" x 7½" strip for bottom fence rail, and two ¾" x 3½" strips for fence posts.
3. From red print fabric, cut a 2½" square for rooster comb/wattle.

4. From gold print fabric, cut a 4" square for rooster body.
5. From gold check fabric, cut a 2" square for rooster wing.
6. Cut all red print, gold print, and gold check squares in half diagonally to form triangles.
7. Cut one 2½" strip across Checkered Border fabric.

APPLIQUÉ AND ASSEMBLY

1. Fuse the appliqué pieces to the background referring to photograph on page 114 and directions below.
2. Place background "on point" and fuse top fence rail 5" from the bottom point. Fuse the bottom fence rail ¾" under the top rail. Center the two fence posts 2½" apart; fuse. Machine-appliqué fence.
3. Center and fuse wing to rooster body. Fuse comb/wattle and wing/body; appliqué rooster.
4. Stem-stitch tail feathers and long-stitch legs and toes with gold embroidery floss. Sew on a ⅜" button for eye.
5. Layer front, two batting squares, and back. Sew just inside edges. Quilt sound waves near beak.
6. Refer to the General Instructions on page 7 to bind the pot holder.
7. Sew a plastic ring 1" to back top point for a hanger (Diagram E).

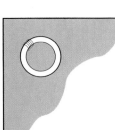

DIAGRAM E

TOASTER COVER

For a toaster cover to crow about, let your imagination run wild with complementary fabrics and fun appliqués like the hen and her chicks!

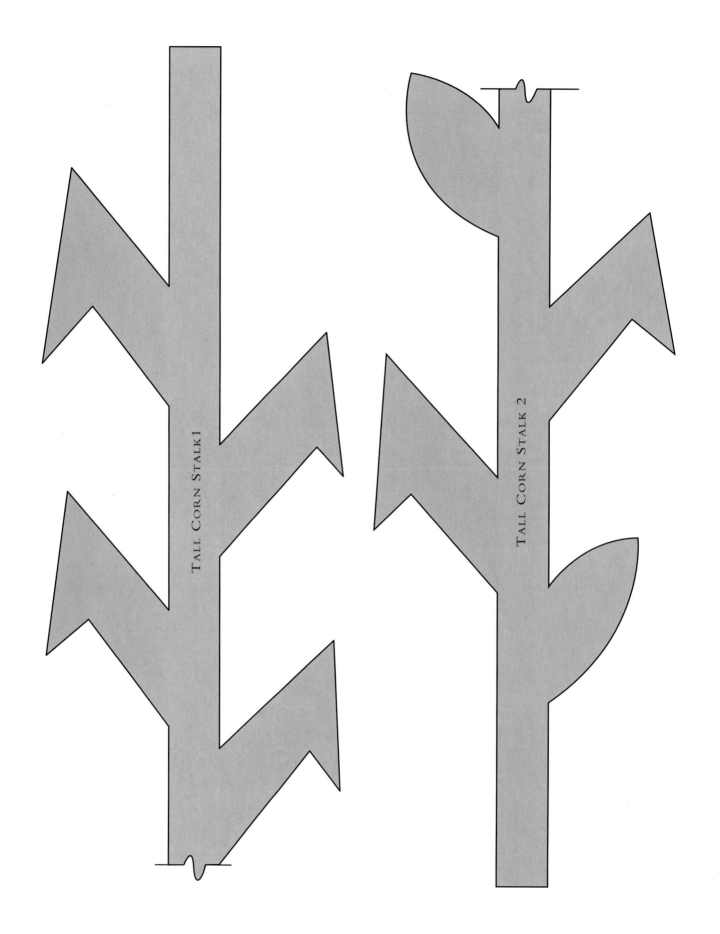

Tall Corn Stalk1

Tall Corn Stalk 2

EGG

SHORT CORN STALK

MEDIUM CORN STALK

Suellen Wassem & Shery Jespersen

Suellen Wassem and Shery Jespersen met in Dayton, Ohio about nine years ago and then began "cahootinizing" on a variety of projects for national publication.

In spite of Shery's move to Wyoming where she lives with her husband, Lynn, a rancher, her venture with Suellen has survived. Shery's designs are now inspired by her life—a patchwork made up of friends, family, ranching, crafting, horses, and being hopelessly in love with the "sweetest cowboy to ever jingle a spur." With all her "goings on," Shery is thankful for having a no-nonsense partner: "If it were not for Suellen, my designs would have been preserved for all time on paper only—indeed two heads are better than one!"

Suellen, wife of a retired Air Force officer and mother of two grown children, has taught many needlework and quilting classes since 1978, and published several books and patterns, too, through her company—Pieceful Hearts Designs. Suellen feels "very blessed" that even though many miles separate them, she and Shery still share a love of folk art design. "Lives are bound to change, but not the ties that bind. Friendship has no season!"

MATERIALS

- ½ yard of red check fabric for background and binding
- ⅓ yard of ecru "tea stain" print fabric for appliqué background fabric
- ⅓ yard of brown plaid fabric for border
- Assorted fabric scraps in brown, blue, red, and green check and white, gold, red, brown, black, and green print for appliqué
- Fusible web
- 1 yard of unbleached muslin for backing
- 26" x 28" batting
- Black pearl cotton
- 4 assorted 1" beige buttons
- 3½" black buttons
- 2½" off-white buttons
- 2½" tan buttons

Quick-Sew Wallhanging

Finished size 24" x 26"

CUTTING

1. From red check background fabric, cut two 6½" x 8½" rectangles, two 6½" x 10½" rectangles, and three 2¾" strips across width of fabric for the binding.

2. From ecru background fabric, cut four 6½" squares and one 8½" x 10½" rectangle.

3. From the brown plaid border fabric cut two 2¾" x 20½" strips and two 2¾" x 27" strips.

4. Refer to the General Instructions, page 6, to trace, apply fusible web and cut out the following appliqué pieces on pages 123–125: Snowman and arms, scarf, broom stick and broom head, ginger-bread cookie cutter kid, stocking and cuff, mitten and heart, and cardinal, beak, and branch.

1. Sew the quilt together referring to Diagram A and the directions that follow:

2. Sew the background pieces together in horizontal strips, two squares and one rectangle for the top and bottom strips and three rectangles for the center strip. Sew strips together.

3. Sew short border strips to top and bottom of pieced center; press seam allowances toward strips.

4. Sew long border strips to the side edges of the pieced center. Press seam allowances toward strips.

5. Referring to photograph on page 119 and directions below, fuse appliqué pieces to the ecru background, layering as indicated by small dashed lines on pattern pieces.

6. For the snowman, fuse broom head first, then the body. Fuse the large arm in place, then the scarf. Fuse the broom handle in place, then fuse the small arm.

7. For the mitten, position the heart on top of the mitten and then fuse both to the background square.

8. For the cardinal, fuse the branch to the background square, then position the body and fuse, then the beak.

9. For the stocking, position the stocking and cuff, then fuse both in place.

10. Fuse the gingerbread kid in place.

11. Using black pearl cotton, blanket stitch around edges of appliqué pieces.

12. Using black pearl cotton make French knots on the snowman's face for eyes, mouth, and nose. Use short running stitches to indicate the straw on the broom.

13. Referring to "Sewing on Buttons" on page 83 and the Xs on the patterns for placement, sew black buttons onto the snowman, a tan button each onto the heart and stocking, and an off-white button onto each gingerbread kid.

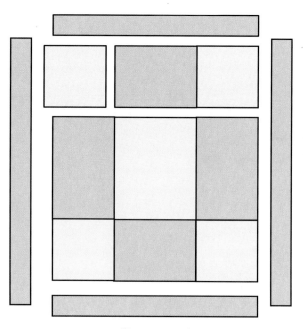

DIAGRAM A

FINISHING

1. Refer to the General Instructions on page 7 to layer the wallhanging.

2. Using black pearl cotton and running stitches, sew diagonal lines from corner to opposite corner in red-and-black check rectangles. Sew a beige button to each intersection in these rectangles.

3. Using black pearl cotton and running stitches, sew just inside the outer edges of the pieced center.

4. Sew the three 2¾" binding strips together end to end. Fold and press long strip wrong sides together.

5. Pin binding strip against backing with raw edges matching. Referring to the General Instructions on page 7 for mitering corners, sew binding in place using a ¼" seam allowance.

6. Turn binding to front; pin in place. Using black pearl cotton thread and large running stitches, secure front of binding to quilt about ⅛" from the folded binding edge.

Gingerbread Garland

Finished size 40" in length

MATERIALS

- Assorted fabric scraps (4"x 5") in brown, red, blue, and green plaid, and gold, red and light brown print for appliqué
- Seven 4" x 5" pieces of felt in brown, red, green, and blue
- Fusible web
- Brown, red, and black embroidery floss
- 11 assorted colors of ½" buttons
- 1⅓ feet of red cording

CUTTING

1. Refer to the General Instructions on page 6 to trace, apply fusible web and cut out the following appliqué pieces on pages 124–125: Three hearts, three mittens, and four gingerbread cookie cutter kids.

ASSEMBLY AND FINISHING

1. Referring to the photograph and the directions below and right, fuse appliqué pieces to the felt rectangles, layering as indicated by the dashed lines on the patterns.

2. Fuse gingerbread kids to felt rectangles.

3. Position a heart on top of each mitten; fuse both to the felt rectangle.

4. Cut out about ⅛" larger than the gingerbread kid or mitten.

5. Using embroidery floss, blanket-stitch along the edges of the appliqué pieces.

6. Referring to "Sewing on Buttons" on page 83 and the Xs on the patterns for placement, sew buttons onto the gingerbread kids and hearts.

7. Tie a knot in each end. Make a small hole near the top of each gingerbread kid and mitten. Every 6", tie shapes to the cording with bows of the untwisted cording or red yarn.

Snowman Towel

MATERIALS

- Assorted fabric scraps in brown and green check, gold print, and beige for appliqué
- Fusible web
- Purchased check or plaid homespun towel
- Black pearl cotton

ASSEMBLY

1. Refer to the General Instructions on page 6 to trace, apply fusible web to, and cut out the following appliqué pieces on page 123: Snowman, scarf, broom stick, and broom head.

2. Referring to the photograph on page 121 and the directions below, apply appliqué pieces to the towel, layering as indicated by the dashed lines on the pattern pieces.

3. For the snowman, fuse broom head first, then the body. Fuse the large arm in place, then the scarf. Fuse the broom handle in place, then the small arm.

4. Using black pearl cotton thread, blanket-stitch along exposed edges of all the appliqué pieces.

5. Using black pearl cotton thread, satin-stitch circles on the snowman's front and face for buttons, eyes, nose and mouth (Diagram B).

DIAGRAM B

Holiday Notes and Recipe Cards

MATERIALS

- Oatmeal card stock or heavy paper measuring about 5" x 12" for each card
- Assorted fabric scraps in brown, red, green, and black or other plaids
- Assorted buttons
- Red, light brown and beige pearl cotton

CUTTING

1. Fold the paper stock at the desired size (4" or 5" x 12") and carefully tear on the fold to make a rough edge.

2. Fold the card in half and crease by running a thumbnail along it.

3. Refer to the General Instructions on page 6 to trace and cut out desired appliqué pieces on pages 123–125. The three cards featured here use one each mitten, heart, small heart, gingerbread kid and long stocking.

ASSEMBLY

1. Rub back of fabric appliqué piece with a glue stick, place on the front of the card, and smooth with fingers. If desired, add a small heart to the inside.

2. Decorate the card by sewing on buttons, making ties and bows, sewing running stitches along the bottom edge, and making facial features with pearl cotton thread.

3. Tie pearl cotton or a ½" wide strip of torn fabric as trim at fold.

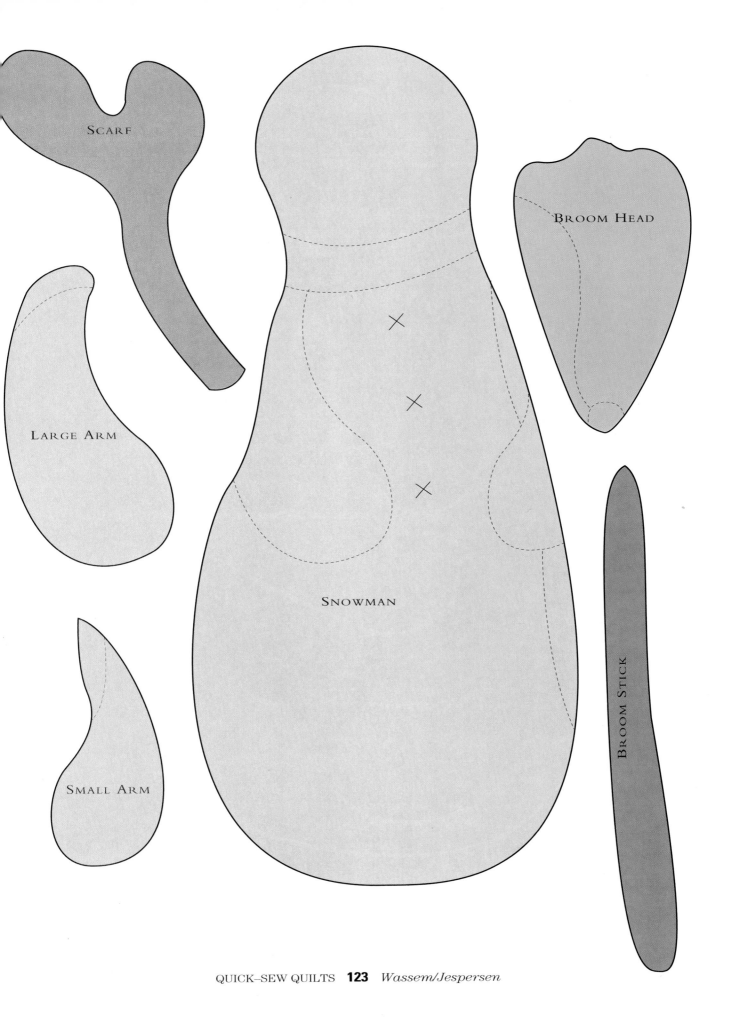

SCARF

BROOM HEAD

LARGE ARM

SNOWMAN

SMALL ARM

BROOM STICK

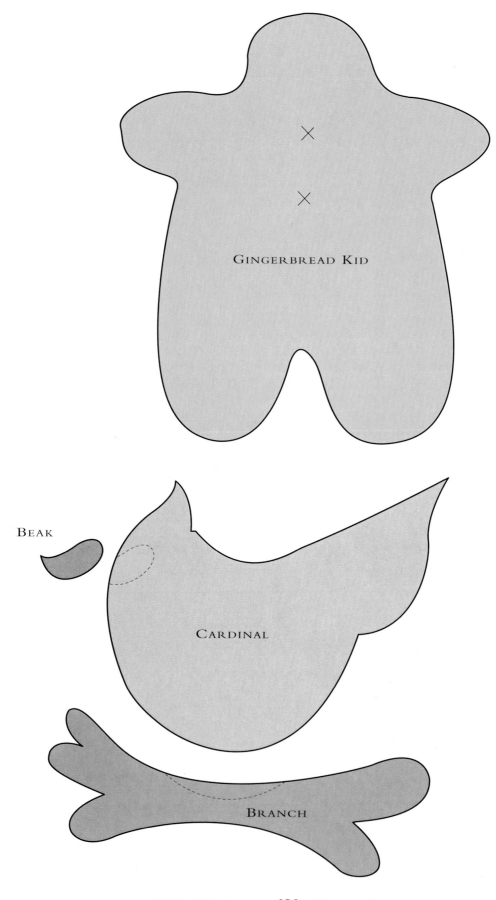

GINGERBREAD KID

BEAK

CARDINAL

BRANCH

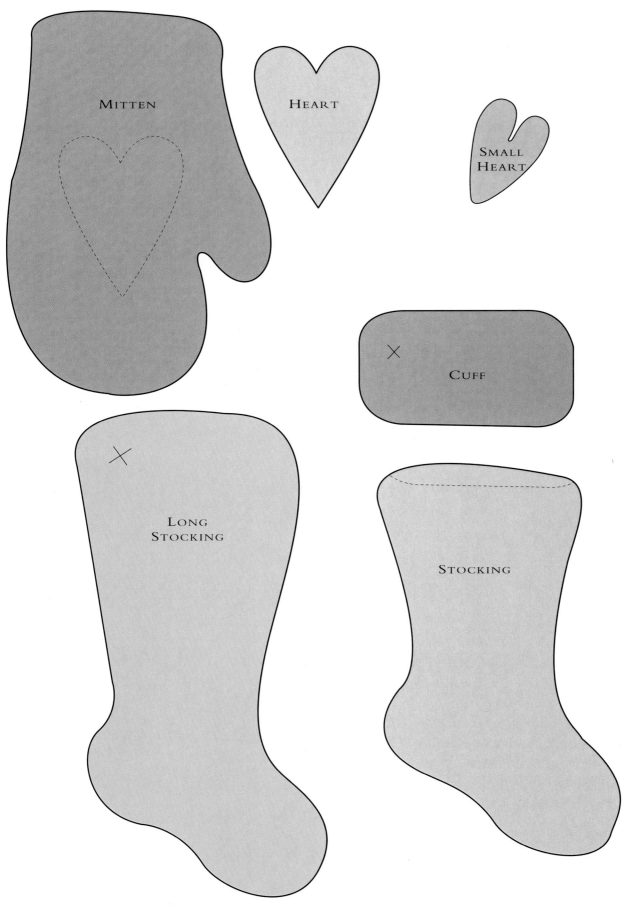

Mitten

Heart

Small Heart

Cuff

Long Stocking

Stocking

Leslie Beck

Talented artist and designer Leslie Beck created her charming Piney Woods wall quilt and whimsical coordinating projects to introduce you to the delights of quick-sew piecing and no-sew appliqué techniques.

Discover for yourself how easy it is to spend an afternoon with Leslie's designs, completing an entire project almost instantly using coordinating country prints and fusible adhesive.

Start with the generously-sized three-panel wallhanging as shown, opposite. Let the featured motifs—a folk Santa, pine trees, and a trio of birdhouses—be your inspiration for a myriad of other projects in Leslie's fresh new quick-sew collection.

On the following pages, you'll find full-size patterns and the complete instructions for making everything from star-studded notecards, a Santa sampler, ornaments and gift bag, to a sweatshirt trimmed with a forest of button-topped pine trees—projects all bursting with the fun and whimsy of Leslie Beck's signature folk-art style!

MATERIALS

- ¾ yard of medium blue print fabric for appliqué background
- ½ yard of red print fabric for border
- ¾ yard of black print fabric for sashing and binding
- 1 yard of fabric for backing
- 36" x 42" batting
- Assorted fabrics in reds, pinks, whites, golds, greens, browns, and black, including prints, plaids, and stripes for appliqué
- Heavyweight fusible web
- Seven assorted red buttons
- Black embroidery floss
- Fine-tip permanent fabric pen

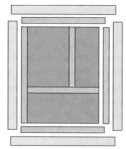

DIAGRAM A

Quick-Sew Wallhanging

Finished size 32" x 39"

CUTTING

1. From blue print fabric, cut one 8" x 20", one 14¾" x 20", and one 10" x 23¾" rectangle.

2. From black print fabric, cut six 2" and four 2¼" strips across the width of the fabric. From 2" strips, cut two 26¾", two 31", one 20", and one 23¾" sashing strips. From 2½" strips, cut two 41" and two 35" binding strips.

3. From red print border fabric, cut four 3" strips across the width of the fabric. From these four strips cut two 31¾" and two 34" border strips.

4. From backing fabric, cut a 36" x 42" rectangle.

5. Refer to the General Instructions on page 6 to trace, apply fusible web to, and cut all appliqué pieces including ¼"-wide strips for birdhouse poles.

PIECING AND ASSEMBLY

1. Sew the quilt top together using Diagram A for reference.

2. Fuse appliqués to pieced top, referring to the photograph and the directions that follow, and layer as indicated by dashed lines on the pattern pieces.

3. Position the top of Santa's face about 2" from top edge of the background. Add the other pieces, adjusting as necessary. Then, fuse from the top layer down. Because of the thickness, it may be necessary to press from the underside.

FINISHING

1. Refer to General Instructions on page 7 to layer, quilt, and bind the wallhanging.

2. Use a fine-tip permanent-ink fabric pen to draw the eyes on Santa, and then draw stitches just inside the beard, hair, and other pieces as desired.

3. Cut four 18" pieces of black floss, tie a knot in each floss tail about ½" from each end. Tie a bow in each piece. Tack one bow to the star on the walking stick and one to each birdhouse.

4. Using black floss, sew a red button to top of each tree except tree with bird. Dot each knot with clear-drying glue.

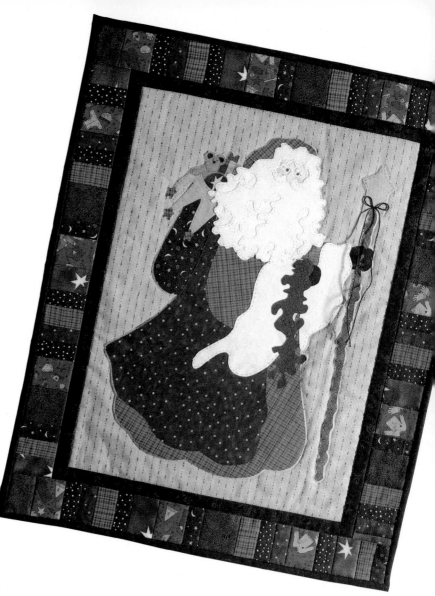

Santa Quilt

Finished size 21" x 26"

MATERIALS

- ⅔ yard of medium brown print fabric for background
- Assorted fabrics in reds, pinks, whites, golds, greens, browns, and black, including prints, plaids, and stripes for Santa appliqué
- Scrap Border, see page 130
- ½ yard of black print fabric for inside border and binding
- ¾ yard of fabric for backing
- 24" x 29" piece of batting
- Heavyweight fusible web
- Black embroidery floss
- Fine-tip permanent fabric pen

CUTTING

1. From brown background fabric, cut a 14¾" x 20" rectangle.

2. From black print fabric, cut two 1¼" strips and four 2½" strips across the width of the fabric. From the 1¼" strips cut two 16¼" and two 20" inside border strips. From the 2½" strips, cut two 27" and two 23" binding strips.

3. For Scrap Border, cut four 2½" strips across the width of the fabric; cut two 20¼" pieces and two 21½" pieces.

4. From the backing fabric, cut a 24" x 29" rectangle.

5. Refer to the General Instructions on page 6 to trace, apply fusible web to, and cut all appliqué pieces on pages 133–138.

PIECING AND ASSEMBLING

1. Sew the quilt top together using Diagram B for reference.
2. After adding Scrap Borders, machine-baste about ⅛" from outer edge.
3. Referring to photograph and layering as indicated by dashed lines on patterns, fuse appliqués to quilt top according to Piecing and Assembly, Step 3, of the Quick-Sew Wallhanging, page 128.

FINISHING

1. Refer to the General Instructions on page 7 to layer, quilt, and bind your wallhanging.
2. Draw eyes on Santa with a fine-tip permanent-ink fabric pen; draw stitches around beard, hair, and where desired.
3. Cut an 18" piece of black floss, tie a knot in each end, and tie a bow. Tack bow to star on walking stick.

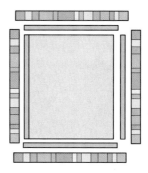

DIAGRAM B

Birdhouse Wall Quilt

Finished size 13" x 25"

MATERIALS

- ¼ yard of black or dark print fabric for background
- ⅛ yard of gold print fabric for inside border
- Assorted fabrics in reds, whites, golds, greens, browns, and blacks, including prints, stripes, and plaids for birdhouse appliqué
- ¼ yard of black print fabric for binding
- Scrap Border, see page 130
- ½ yard fabric for backing
- Heavyweight fusible web
- 17" x 29" piece of batting
- Black embroidery floss
- Fine-tip permanent fabric pen

CUTTING

1. From black or dark print background, cut an 8" x 20" rectangle.
2. From gold print fabric, cut two 1" strips; cut into two 20" and two 9" inside border strips.
3. From Scrap Border cut two 2½" strips; cut two 13" and two 21" pieces.
4. From black print fabric, cut two 2½" strips; cut into two 27" and two 16" binding strips.
5. From backing fabric, cut a 17" x 29" rectangle.
6. Refer to the General Instructions on page 6 to trace, apply fusible web to, and cut all pieces on page 141, including ¼"-wide strips for birdhouse poles.

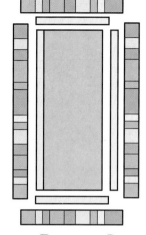

DIAGRAM C

PIECING AND ASSEMBLY

1. Sew the quilt top together using Diagram C for reference, pressing seam allowances to one side.
2. After adding Scrap Borders, machine-baste ⅛" from the outer edge to prevent stretching.
3. Fuse appliqués to pieced top referring to photograph, and layering as indicated by dashed line on the patterns.

FINISHING

1. Refer to the General Instructions on page 7 to layer, quilt, and bind the birdhouse wallhanging.
2. Use a fabric pen to draw the stitches on the snow and the birdhouses.
3. Cut three 18" pieces of black floss. Tie a knot ½" from each end, and tie a bow. Tack one bow under each birdhouse.

SCRAP BORDER

Choose six of the appliqué fabrics or other coordinating fabrics to make the Scrap Border. Cut three 14" strips of each fabric, varying the width of these strips from 1½" to 2½". With right sides together, mixing color and width, and changing sewing directions after sewing each strip, sew the strips together to make a 14" x 22" rectangle. Press all seam allowances in one direction. Using the diagram below for reference, cut strips crosswise as directed for each quilt.

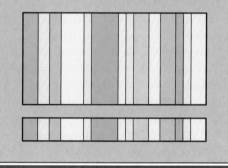

SANTA SAMPLER

Fuse the Santa-head appliqué pieces onto a 9" square of dark fabric. Layer this on 12" squares of star print fabric, fleece batting, and holiday-print backing. Draw stitches inside the appliqué and add decorative running stitches and several buttons. Trim the edges with pinking shears.

Tree Sweatshirt

MATERIALS

- Sweatshirt with set-in sleeves
- Assorted fabrics in greens, brown, and red for trees and bird appliqué
- Heavyweight fusible web
- 28 assorted red buttons
- Black embroidery floss

ADDING DESIGN

1. Pre-wash the sweatshirt and the fabrics. Do not use fabric softener.
2. Refer to the General Instructions on page 6 to trace, apply fusible web to, and cut all appliqué pieces on page 140.
3. Fuse appliqués to sweatshirt referring to photograph.

FINISHING

1. Sew the buttons in place with black embroidery floss, being sure to tie floss off on the top of each button.
2. Dot each knot with clear-drying glue.
3. See Tips & Techniques on page 83, for tips on care of embellished garments.

MATERIALS

- Black, or other color, kraft paper bag with twine or raffia handles
- Assorted fabrics in reds, greens, golds, browns, blacks, and whites for birdhouse appliqués
- Fusible web
- Off-white acrylic paint

DECORATING

1. Refer to the General Instructions on page 6 to trace, apply fusible web to, and cut all appliqué pieces on page 141, including ¼"-wide strips for the birdhouse poles.

2. Fuse appliqués to one side of bag, referring to photograph and layering as indicated by the dashed lines on the patterns.

3. Determine position of the birdhouses; cut the poles to fit from birdhouse to bottom edge of the bag.

4. Using an old toothbrush, fleck bag with off-white acrylic paint. Dilute paint with water to an ink-like consistency. Dip toothbrush into paint, then gently pull a knife edge across bristles, working toward your body to keep paint off yourself. Clean the knife frequently to avoid large spatters on the project. Let dry.

BIRDHOUSE NOTE CARDS

Use the same appliqué and spatter techniques as for the paper bag to decorate personalized note cards.

BIRDHOUSE ORNAMENTS

Fuse the birdhouse appliqué to heavy brown paper. Use pinking shears to cut paper about ¼" outside the appliqué. Decorate with buttons, make a hole near the top and hang with floss or ribbon.

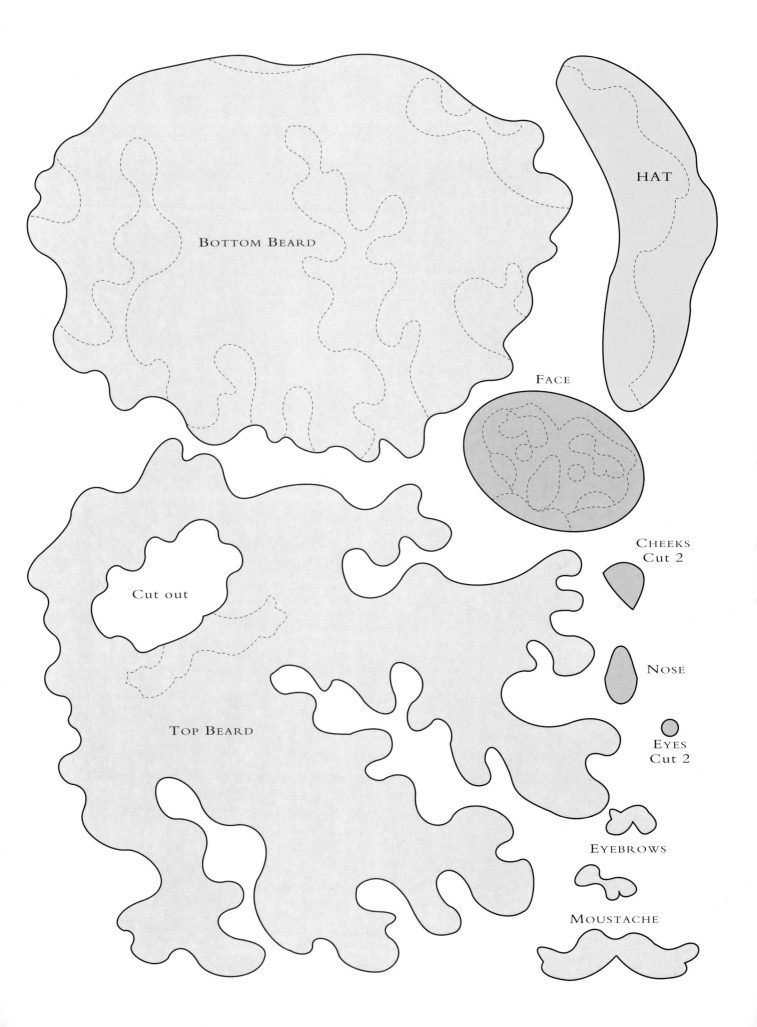

BOTTOM BEARD

HAT

FACE

CHEEKS
Cut 2

Cut out

NOSE

TOP BEARD

EYES
Cut 2

EYEBROWS

MOUSTACHE

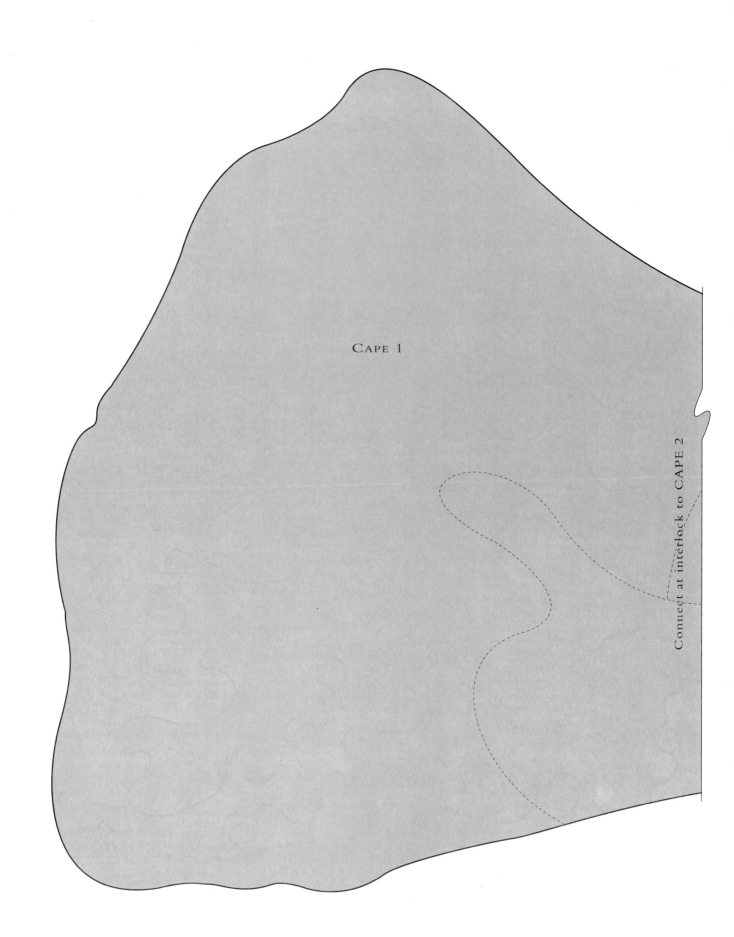

Cape 1

Connect at interlock to CAPE 2

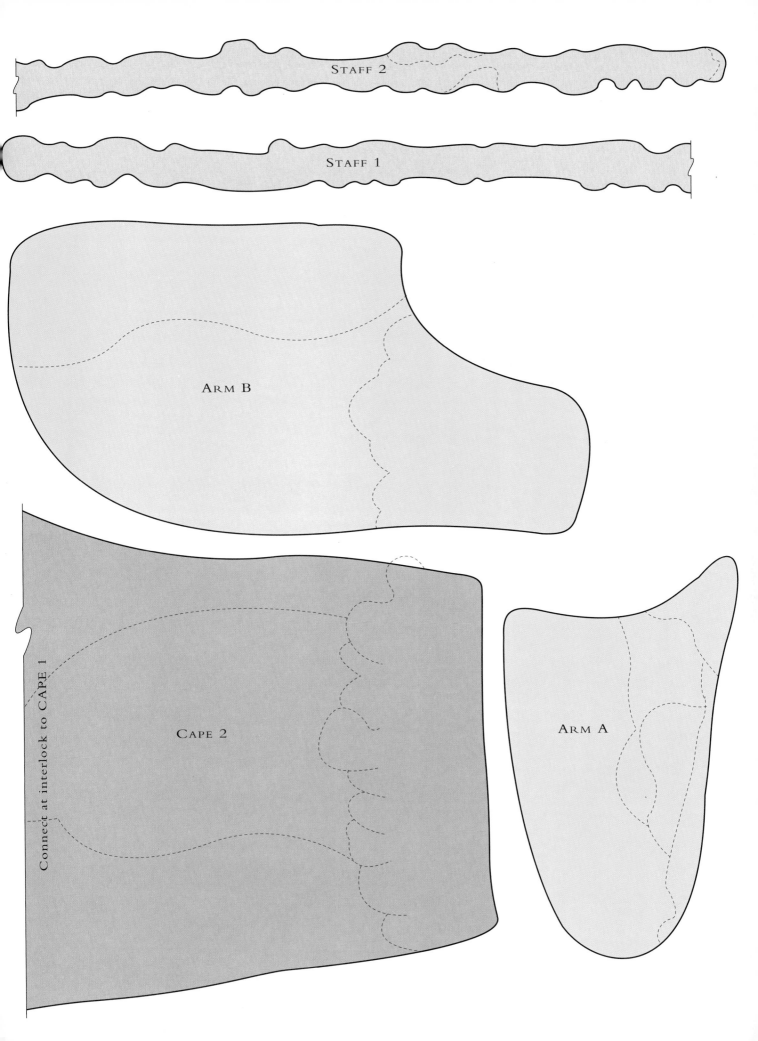

STAFF 2

STAFF 1

ARM B

Connect at interlock to CAPE 1

CAPE 2

ARM A

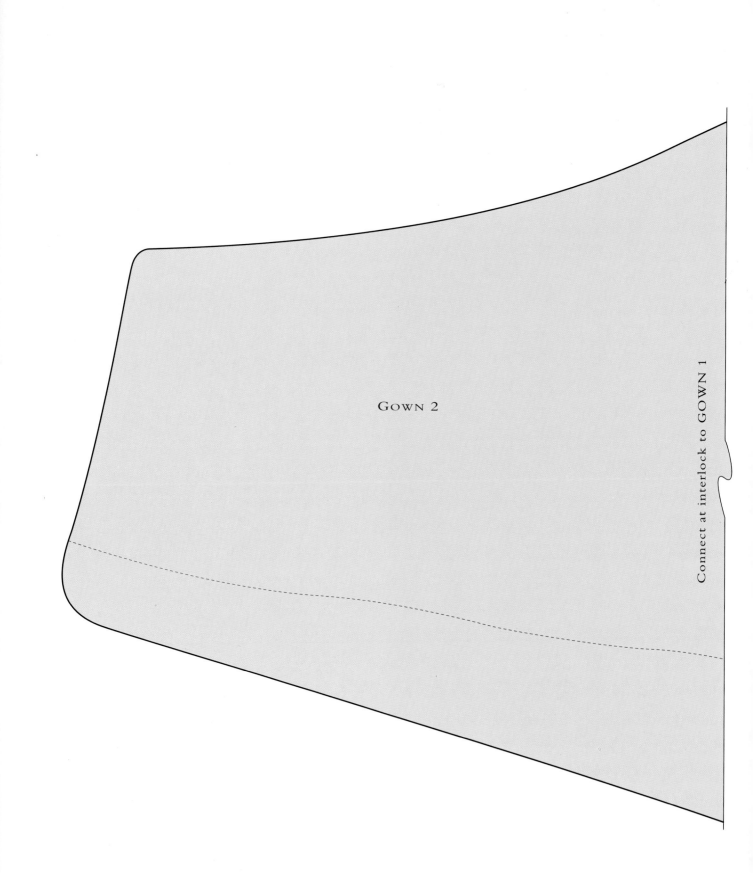

Gown 2

Connect at interlock to GOWN 1

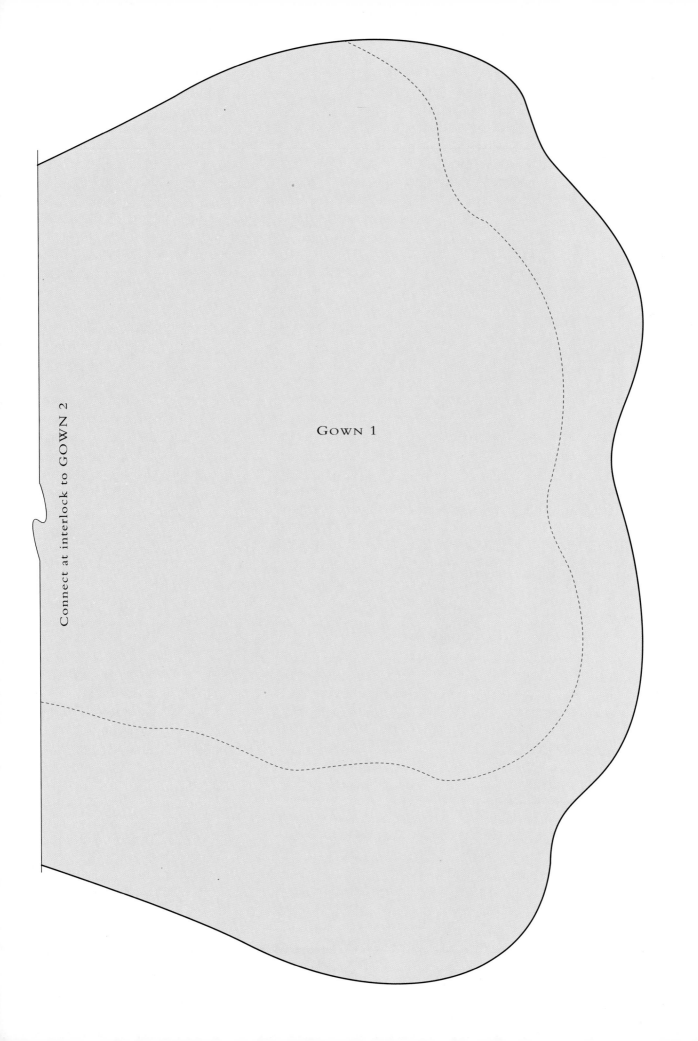

Connect at interlock to GOWN 2

GOWN 1

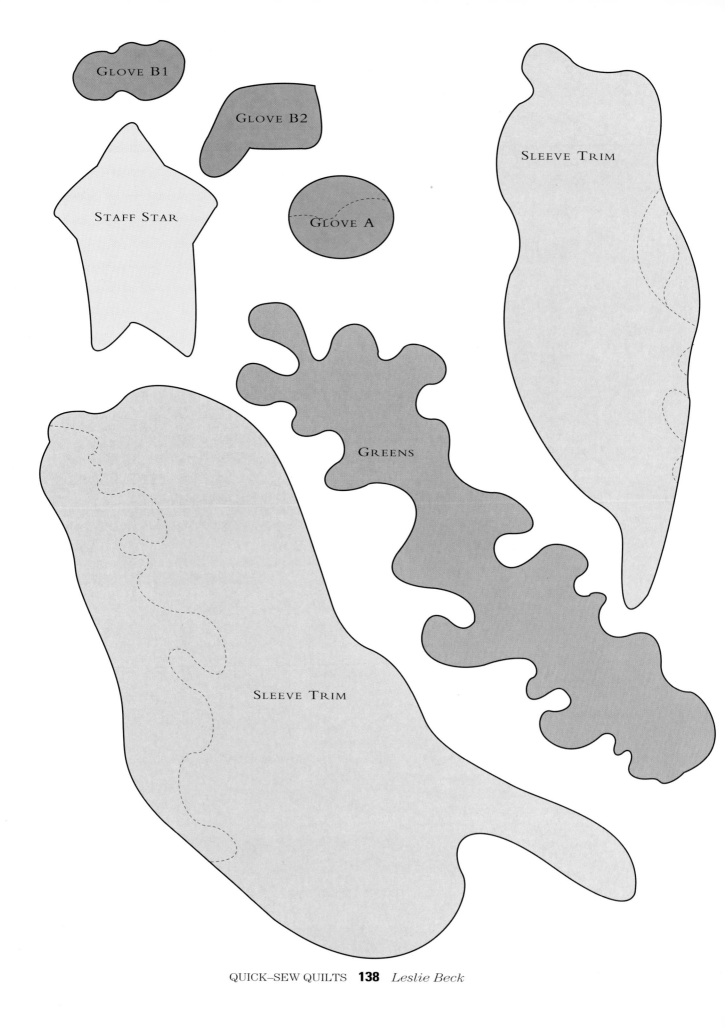

GLOVE B1

GLOVE B2

GLOVE A

STAFF STAR

SLEEVE TRIM

GREENS

SLEEVE TRIM

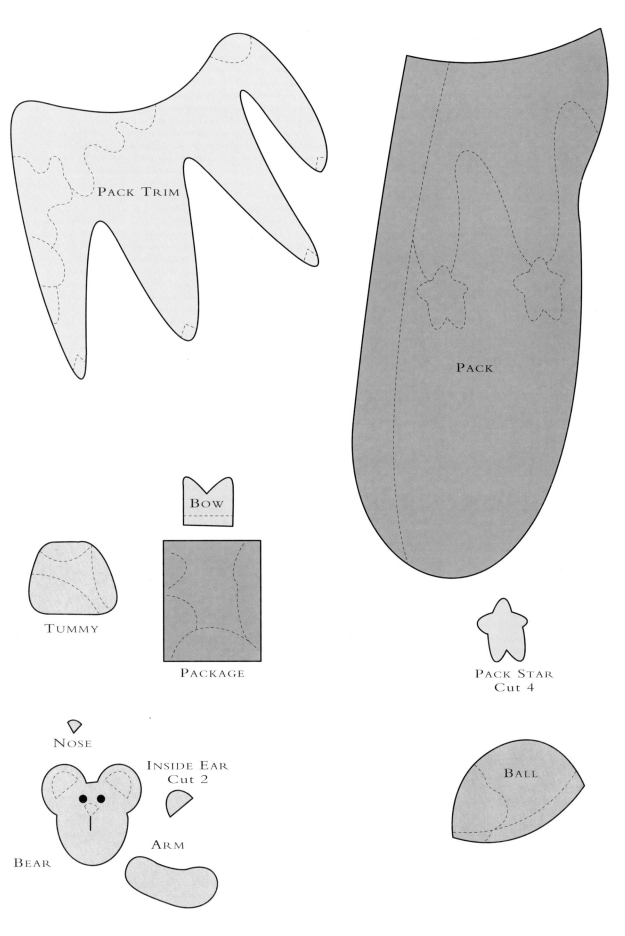

PACK TRIM

PACK

BOW

TUMMY

PACKAGE

PACK STAR
Cut 4

NOSE

INSIDE EAR
Cut 2

BEAR

ARM

BALL

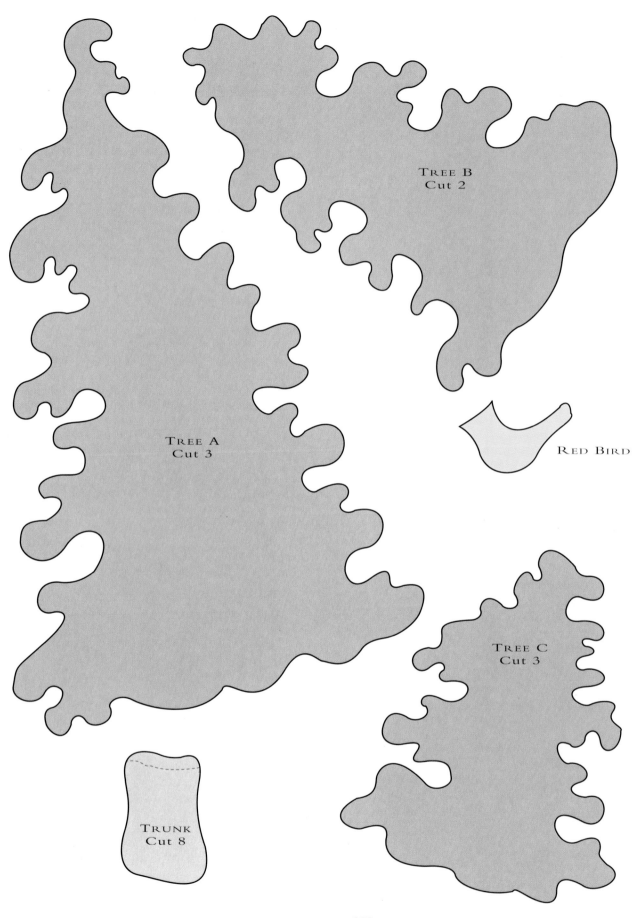

Tree B
Cut 2

Tree A
Cut 3

Red Bird

Tree C
Cut 3

Trunk
Cut 8

B

B

B

A

BIRDHOUSE B

A

B

B

A

A

BIRDHOUSE A

GLOSSARY

APPLIQUÉ As a noun it refers to a piece of fabric that is placed on a background either by sewing or, as instructed many times in this book, by fusing. As a verb, it refers to the process of securing a piece of fabric on the background.

BACKING The bottom layer (back) of a quilt.

BASTING Temporary stitches or pins, holding the quilt layers together.

BATTING The filling between two layers of fabric. It contributes warmth to a quilt, and structure to wallhangings and clothing. Batting comes in a variety of lofts (thicknesses) and fibers (wool, cotton, or polyester, or a combination).

BIAS The diagonal grain of the fabric; usually at a 45° angle to the selvage.

BINDING A fabric strip that encloses the layers at the edge of a quilt.

BORDER One or more fabric strips that frame the center part of a quilt top.

CRAZY QUILT Irregular-shaped pieces sewn onto a foundation fabric, usually embellished with embroidery stitches.

EMBROIDERY Decorative hand- or machine-stitching using thread or yarn.

FUSIBLE WEB A product consisting of a layer of heat sensitive fibers and a paper layer to facilitate construction.

QUILT As a noun it refers to a top layered with batting and backing and held together with stitches. As a verb it refers to the process of securing the layers with small hand- or machine-stitches and is usually done in a pattern.

REVERSE To turn a pattern over to cut the design in the opposite direction.

SEAM ALLOWANCE The space between the stitching line and the edge of the fabric.

TEMPLATE A pattern made from plastic or cardboard, used as a guide for marking and transferring the pattern shape onto fabric by tracing around it.

SOURCES

Our featured designers are a wonderful resource for additional patterns, materials, and supplies. You are welcome to contact each at the address and phone number included below.

Lynette Jensen—*Courthouse Pines*
Thimbleberries' fabrics designed by Lynette are by RJR Fashion Fabrics. For a catalog of patterns and books, send $2 to: Thimbleberries, 205 Jefferson Street, Department LB, Hutchinson, MN 55350; 612/587-3944.

Margaret Sindelar—*Bluebird of Happiness Sampler*
The fabrics Margaret Sindelar used are from the Variations Collection by Concord House, a Division of Concord Fabrics (212/760-0343). She used DMC quilting threads and floss, and batting from Morning Glory Products, a Division of Carpenter Company (800/234-9105). Choosing from more than 3,000 possible stitch variations, Margaret created the appliqué treatment on the jacket using the Viking #1+ Sewing Machine (800/446-2333). Cottonwood Classics, 4813 Cody Drive, West Des Moines, IA 50265; 515/225-8409.

Sandy Belt—*Animals Two by Two*
Sandy used Kunin Felt (800/292-7900) for some of her projects. For the kid's felt vest, she used Pattern IJ344 from Indygo Junction (913/341-5559). Town Folk Designs, 6612 U.S. 41 South, Marquette, MI 49855; 906/249-1898.

Sally Korte and Alice Strebel—*Forever Friends*
Sally and Alice use an eclectic blend of fabrics and notions for their whimsical fashions. For a catalog of clothing, quilting and crafting patterns, send $3 to: Kindred Spirits, 115 Colonial Lane, Dayton, OH 45429; 513/435-7758.

Patrice Longmire—*From My Heart to Yours*
Patterns for Patrice's quilting and crafting projects include her one-of-a kind doll patterns. For a catalog, send $2 to: Patrice & Company, 152 East 11th Avenue, Escondido, CA 92025; 619/743-7528.

McKenna Ryan—*Cabin Creek*
Moose and other finials and numerous "Northwoods" patterns packaged in McKenna Ryan's distinctive brown paper bag with raffia ties are available from Pine Needles. For a catalog, send $2 to: Pine Needles, 247 Lake Blaine Drive, Kalispell, MT 59901; 406/752-6086.

Janet Pittman—*From My Mother's Garden*
Janet Pittman's collection features a variety of Hoffman Fabrics (800/547-0100). The vest is quilted denim from Dan River. Janet used Sulky's rayon thread for the embellishments. Garden Trellis Designs, 2717 Scenic Place, West Des Moines, IA 50265; 515/223-6735.

Cheryl Jukich—*String Fling*
The featured winter wonderland vest is part of a series of patterns for interchangeable vests and quilted wearables from Cheryl Jukich's "Quik-Quilt"™ series—a technique showing how to turn a humble sweatshirt into a quilted garment using no batting or lining. All specialty buttons (wood and hand-painted porcelain) may be ordered from her company. For a color catalog and subscription to "Barefacts" newsletter, send $6 to: Threadbare Pattern Company, Dept. C, P.O. Box 1484, Havelock, NC 28532; 800/4-PATTERN.

Kris Kerrigan—*Something to Crow About*
Kris Kerrigan's kitchen collection and other patterns are inspired by familiar scenes of fields of corn, fence rows, and a menagerie of animals on the family farm. For a catalog, send $2 to: BUTTON WEEDS, 1275 Pheasant Avenue, Afton, IA 50830; 515/347-8831.

Suellen Wassem and Shery Jespersen—*Winter Wonderland*
Suellen Wassem and Shery Jespersen used DMC pearl cotton and floss. Several of Suellen's project books offer additional patterns for wallhangings featuring light-hearted snowmen, mitten, and star projects. For a catalog, send $2 to: Pieceful Heart Designs, 2715 East Tara Trail, Beavercreek, OH 45434-6256; 513/320-9003.

Leslie Beck—*Piney Woods*
Leslie uses fabrics she designed for V.I.P. Fabrics. Many of Leslie's patterns feature her signature Santas and garden angels. For a catalog, send $2 to: Fiber Mosaics, 6855 W. Clearwater, Suite K, Kennewick, WA 99336; 509/735-1463.

PROJECT INDEX